AFTER TRAGEDY AND TRIUMPH

Essays in Modern Jewish Thought
and the American Experience

BOOKS BY MICHAEL BERENBAUM

The Vision of the Void: Theological Reflections on the Works of Elie Wiesel (1979)

Report to the President, The President's Commission on the Holocaust (1979)

From Holocaust to New Life (1983)

Holocaust: Religious and Philosophical Implications [With John K. Roth] (1989)

After Tragedy and Triumph: Essays in Modern Jewish Thought and the American Experience (1990)

A Mosaic of Victims (1990)

After Tragedy and Triumph

❖❖❖❖❖❖❖❖❖❖❖❖❖❖❖

Essays in Modern Jewish Thought and the American Experience

MICHAEL BERENBAUM

Hymen Goldman {Adjunct} Professor of Theology
Georgetown University

Project Director
The United States Holocaust Memorial Museum

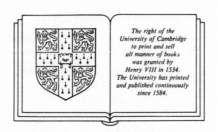

The right of the University of Cambridge to print and sell all manner of books was granted by Henry VIII in 1534. The University has printed and published continuously since 1584.

CAMBRIDGE UNIVERSITY PRESS

Cambridge

New York   Port Chester   Melbourne   Sydney

Published by the Press Syndicate of the University of Cambridge
The Pitt Building, Trumpington Street, Cambridge CB2 1RP
40 West 20th Street, New York, NY 10011, USA
10 Stamford Road, Oakleigh, Melbourne 3166, Australia

First published 1990

Printed in the United States of America

Library of Congress Cataloging-in-Publication Data

Berenbaum, Michael, 1945–

After tragedy and triumph : essays in modern Jewish thought and
the American experience / Michael Berenbaum.

p.   cm.

ISBN 0-521-38057-X

1. Holocaust, Jewish (1939–1945) – Public opinion.   2. Public
opinion – Jews.   3. Public opinion – United States.   4. Jews – United
States – Attitudes.   5. Judaism – 20th century.   I. Title.
D804.3.B46   1991   90–36149
940.53'18 – dc20   CIP

British Library Cataloguing in Publication Data

Berenbaum, Michael 1945–

After tragedy and triumph : essays in Modern Jewish
thought and the American experience.

1. United States. Judaism, history
I. Title
296.0973

ISBN 0-521-38057-X hardback

IN MEMORY OF MY FATHER

Saul Berenbaum, z'l

15 Shevat 5670 – 10 Tevet 5750

IN HONOR OF MY MOTHER

Rhea Berenbaum
As the years of her life move toward
the years of her strength
(Psalm 34)

IN GRATITUDE

My parents have been there for me again and again
with grace and with dignity

Contents

Foreword

Michael Berenbaum is a new and unique phenomenon among contemporary Jewish religious thinkers. He is an intellectual professional working for the U.S. government and a committed, religiously observant Jew. Having made his home in the capital city of the United States for more than a decade, he has an informed and sophisticated understanding of the way that very special city functions. He has worked in the White House. He is well acquainted with Congress, the city's think tanks, newspapers, lawyers, lobbyists, and religious and cultural institutions, as well as the federal bureaucracy. Unlike England, France, and Japan, the United States has two capitals: New York, the media, financial, and commercial capital; and Washington, the political capital. Both are international cities, but with very different cultures. New York has by far the larger Jewish population, actually the world's largest Jewish population, reflecting the fact that Jews have traditionally been more involved in finance, commerce, and the media world than in the world of power and command. By contrast, a goodly part of Washington's Jewish population is involved in one or another aspect of the business of government.

There is nothing accidental about Berenbaum's choice of domicile. He is a Jewish thinker with a very special academic and vocational history. He has served under President Jimmy Carter as Deputy Director of the President's Commission on the Holocaust. The Commission was charged with recommending a national Holocaust memorial. Currently, Berenbaum serves as Project Director of the United States Holocaust Memorial Museum that is being built in Washington. He also teaches at Georgetown University, an institution that itself derives much of its distinctiveness from its Washington location.

As Berenbaum explains in the chapter on "The Nativization of the Holocaust," although privately funded, the U.S. Holocaust

Memorial Museum is a government institution. Berenbaum has played a significant role in formulating the way that institution can be expected to interpret to the American public the greatest single catastrophe in all of Jewish history. Because of the nonsectarian character of the museum's sponsorship, it must present the Holocaust in a way that is meaningful to all Americans of goodwill while maintaining strict fidelity to the historical facts. Berenbaum has played a leading role in this endeavor, transcending ethnic parochialism in his understanding and interpretation of the principal events and issues of contemporary Judaism. This is apparent in the character of his religious thinking, which is profoundly committed to Jewish tradition and thoroughly imbued with the American experience.

The intellectual and spiritual odyssey that brought Berenbaum to his present vocation has also been distinctive. He received a thorough grounding in biblical and rabbinic Judaism at New York's Ramaz Yeshiva and Jerusalem's Hebrew University. His choice of graduate school was, however, very different from that normally elected by American scholars preparing for a career in Jewish studies. Usually, that path leads to one of the major American-Jewish seminaries and then to such institutions as Harvard, Brown, Columbia, or the University of Chicago in addition to a period of study in Israel, usually at the Hebrew University. Although Berenbaum did study at the Hebrew University, he elected to pursue his doctoral studies at a Southern university, Florida State University, whose student body and faculty are overwhelmingly conservative Protestants. Berenbaum's academic experience in Tallahassee thus brought him into contact with a very different academic community than he would have encountered in Cambridge, New Haven, New York, or Chicago. It also brought him closer to heartland America. At the same time, a portion of his graduate years were spent in study at Florida State's Centro Studio in Florence, Italy.

Nevertheless, Berenbaum did not come south to neglect his primary commitment. He was one of the earliest Jewish scholars to grasp the importance of Elie Wiesel as a preeminent religious and theological figure. His doctoral dissertation, *The Vision of the Void: Theological Reflections on the Work of Elie Wiesel,* was subse-

quently published in revised form by Wesleyan University Press.[1]
In assessing the way Wiesel communicates his experience of the
Holocaust, Berenbaum was preparing for his own encounter with
the problem of how the story is to be told and what meaning it is
to have for the larger community, both Jewish and non-Jewish.

Berenbaum's academic sojourn in Tallahassee contributed much
toward his development as an *American* Jewish thinker. In the past,
Jewish thinkers who were at home in the American mainstream
tended to lack a traditional Jewish background. Not so Berenbaum, who is at home within both the American mainstream and
the Jewish tradition.

It was Hegel who said that every thinker is a child of his time.
That is certainly true of Berenbaum. Born the year World War II
came to an end, his formative years were the 1960s. Unlike Holocaust theologians such as Emil Fackenheim, Yitzchak Greenberg,
Arthur Cohen, and myself, for whom World War II was *the* war
of our lifetime, whatever else we experienced, Berenbaum's wars
were Vietnam, the Six Day War of 1967, the Yom Kippur War of
1973, and, above all, the War in Lebanon of 1982–84. As Berenbaum observes in his introduction, the story told by the Holocaust
theologians of my generation was one of death and rebirth. Each
of us had experienced the horror of the Holocaust as a *contemporary*
event even when we were safely removed from its actual occur-
rence. When, against all odds, the State of Israel was founded and
when the Six Day War of 1967 ended with the whole of the land
in Israel's possession, instead of the utter destruction promised by
the Arabs, we were overjoyed by the incredible rebirth. As Raul
Hilberg has observed, the State of Israel was our great consolation
for the *Shoah*.

Today we understand that the story of the Holocaust and the
State of Israel is far too complex to be told primarily as a mythic
saga of death and rebirth. Assuredly, there was rebirth, but rebirth
to all of the harsh realities that currently confront Israel and its
people.

Berenbaum's essays therefore constitute a further elaboration of
the quest for religious self-understanding within the Jewish community, one that is both relevant and appropriate to our time.
As Berenbaum tells us, this book addresses three central issues:

(1) the Jewish identity after the Holocaust and after the birth of the State of Israel; (2) the tensions created within the Jewish tradition between the history of victimization and the assumption of power; (3) the options confronting free Jewish communities in the wake of decreased antisemitism.

The American-Jewish response to the Holocaust constitutes a central theme in Berenbaum's religious thought. Berenbaum includes in this volume dialogues with Arnold Jacob Wolf and David Weiss respectively. Both writers deny the centrality of the Holocaust to contemporary Judaism. Although Berenbaum argues convincingly for the centrality of the Holocaust, his most decisive reason is entirely nonparochial and reflects his service in the city of Washington. Berenbaum tells us, "I fear the Holocaust may become a new threshold, a precedent for what people can do to each other. That is the most important reason we must share the lessons of the Holocaust, integrating them into our collective being so that we can become sensitive to danger signals and effective in prevention."

Moreover, as a religious thinker for whom the 1960s were formative years, Berenbaum offers a new reading of the writings of Franz Rosenzweig and Martin Buber in his chapter "Franz Rosenzweig and Martin Buber Reconsidered." Berenbaum's reading takes issue with the way these thinkers were understood in the sixties. In August 1966 *Commentary* published a symposium on "The Condition of Jewish Belief."[2] In his introduction to the symposium, Milton Himmelfarb observed that Franz Rosenzweig was "the single greatest influence on the religious thought of North American Jewry." Shortly before the symposium appeared, Chaim Potok had written, also in *Commentary*, of Martin Buber's almost total lack of influence among his own people.[3] Berenbaum argues that Buber has far more to say to contemporary Jews than does Rosenzweig, who, by his elevation of Jewish powerlessness to a divinely sanctioned condition necessary for the redemption of humanity, legitimated and thus helped perpetuate the conditions that led to Jewish victimization.

Buber and Rosenzweig had very different attitudes toward Jewish law. Many of the thinkers queried in the *Commentary* symposium valued Rosenzweig largely because of his project of entering

Jewish life from the periphery as an assimilated Jew and seeking to become ever more observant, albeit with a nontraditional rationale for observance. Buber, by contrast, was without commitment to the observance of the Law. He did not share the traditional view that the Torah's commandments were communicated by God at Sinai to the Jewish people, who were thereafter obligated to their fulfillment. He regarded the revelation at Sinai as the I–Thou encounter par excellence in which God's *ineffable* presence was experienced directly. For Buber, the commandments were already an attempt to reduce the ineffability of the supreme encounter to humanly manageable and predictable dimensions. That which had been the supreme I–Thou encounter was reduced to the objectifying distortions of I–"it."

The Jewish thinkers who responded to the *Commentary* symposium tended to regard Buber's treatment of the Law as unacceptably anarchic. Although I was perhaps the most radical thinker among the respondents, it was my belief that the Law took on greater rather than lesser significance after Auschwitz. Although not personally observant, I argued that *all* of the Torah is holy. As the inheritance of the House of Jacob, it obligates every Jew in every generation to decide which commandments he or she will observe.[4] In the aftermath of Auschwitz, the possibility of an I–Thou relation to Divinity did not seem credible to me. All that remained was the Law.

By contrast, Berenbaum had experienced the radical relativizing of life styles that was so much a part of the culture of the 1960s. While personally committed to religious observance, Berenbaum found Buber's attempt to meet God unencumbered by the constraints of structure or tradition meaningful in a way that the earlier thinkers could not. This does not mean that Berenbaum sees Buber as a thoroughgoing religious anarchist or that Berenbaum endorses such anarchy. As Berenbaum points out, Buber recognized that life is lived "between the poles of structured and unstructured experience." Nevertheless, for Berenbaum as for Buber, the supreme moments of renewal are the unpredictable and admittedly "dangerous and fragile dimension of experience, which Buber called I–You."

Those who, like Berenbaum, regard the moments of meeting

as the moments of renewal are predisposed to pluralism in religious life. Berenbaum's Washington experience is an additional factor in such a predisposition, leading him to reflect upon the single most important religious transformation in Jewish life since the sixties, the renaissance of Orthodox Judaism. Berenbaum observes that when he was growing up, traditional Judaism was plagued by a sense of erosion. That is no longer the case. Contemporary American Orthodoxy is imbued with a sense of confidence, legitimacy, and power. In Israel Orthodoxy's claim to exclusive legitimacy has been almost completely accepted by the state and Orthodox religious parties have achieved a virtual monopoly over religious life.

While Berenbaum finds much to admire in Orthodoxy, he nevertheless sees its power as matched by what he regards as a dangerous insularity. It is possible for Orthodox Jews in Israel to attend school, serve in the army, and live in neighborhoods in which they have only a minimal contact with secular Jews and the secular culture. In earlier decades Orthodox Judaism was compelled by the tragic circumstances of Jewish history to cooperate with Reform, Conservative, and secularist Jews. As its power has increased, Orthodoxy has tended to become less disposed to such cooperation either in Israel or in the diaspora.

An irreparable breach in the unity of the Jewish people was inconceivable to the Holocaust theologians. After Auschwitz every Jewish resource was devoted to rescue and renewal. Neither energy nor resources were available for divisive religious strife. Unfortunately, there has always been a theological basis for such strife in Orthodoxy's claim to exclusive truth and authority. Strictly speaking, Orthodoxy does not regard Reform and Conservative Judaism as legitimate Jewish religious alternatives but as movements that have legitimated rebellion against the divinely bestowed commandments. In an era of radical communal dislocation, a weakened Orthodoxy was willing to cooperate on matters of rescue with the then more powerful non-Orthodox movements. That, however, was an interim tactic and, as Berenbaum suggests, there is reason to believe that the period of accommodation is coming to an end. If it does, the Jewish people will be threatened with the worst kind of schism, that which is religiously legitimated and brooks no compromise.

According to Berenbaum, the Orthodox renaissance is due at least in part to the failure of much of the Zionist vision in spite of Zionism's extraordinary achievements. Berenbaum observes that Zionism envisaged the establishment of the State of Israel as leading to the normalization of Jewish life, genuine political independence for the state, the ingathering of the exiles of the diaspora, and the end to Jewish vulnerability, none of which has taken place. The failed vision has resulted in a meaning-vacuum that messianic and sectarian groups within Israeli Orthodoxy propose to fill.

Given the catastrophic events that have afflicted world Jewry since the 1881 pogroms in czarist Russia and that have included the mass emigration of Eastern European Jewry, the Holocaust, the birth and the continuing travail of the State of Israel, it is by no means surprising that Jewish history has been interpreted messianically and apocalyptically by such radical movements as Gush Emunim. Even secular Zionists ascribed a redemptive meaning to the birth of the State of Israel, although they were not prepared to base their politics on a messianic-apocalyptic reading of Jewish history. Orthodox sectarians are prepared so to do. They see the Holocaust, the State of Israel, and the occupation of all of the land of Israel as indispensable preludes to the final messianic climax of Jewish history. Such an ideology fosters a militant unwillingness to compromise on any accommodation with the Palestinians. It also nurtures the faith that religiously compliant, spiritually prepared Jews need have no fear of the outcome of the final military conflict between Israel and the enemies surrounding her. Unfortunately, the last Jews who were convinced that the Lord would fight with Israel against her enemies were the Zealots in their suicidal rebellion against Rome. Berenbaum concludes his book with the grim observation that there is a strong possibility that the tensions of the region will lead to "apocalyptic politics."

In conclusion, having pointed to the differences between Berenbaum's thought and that of the Holocaust theologians, I would caution against positing too great a distinction between Berenbaum and their current thought and sensibility. Although the Holocaust theologians were shaped intellectually and spiritually by very different historical experiences, they have been sensitive to the transformations in the Jewish situation that have occurred in the 1970s and 1980s. Berenbaum has identified me as his teacher, and it is an old and honored Jewish tradition that the wise teacher learns from his student. If my ideas about Jews and Judaism have not been frozen at a particular moment in time, much of the credit is due to what I have learned from my student Michael Berenbaum.

RICHARD L. RUBENSTEIN

Introduction

These essays, written over the past several years, address three central issues: the identity of Jews after the tragedy of the Holocaust and the triumph of Israel, the tensions created within Jewish tradition between a history of victimization and the assumption of power, and the choices facing free Jewish communities in the wake of decreased antisemitism. After the Holocaust, Jews recast their role in history, assuming political power and linking religious survival with the fate of a secular state.

Unlike their European ancestors, American Jews live in freedom, outside physical or intellectual ghettos. Jews can no longer speak one way to the community and another to those beyond the circle of faith. Jewish intellectuals enjoy the liberty and self-confidence to ask painful questions and face the consequences. At home in American society, American Jews – committed to their religious and ethnic heritage – are wrestling with the twin revolutions of modern Jewish experience, which are seemingly antithetical.

Two critical European philosophers, Friedrich Nietzsche and Jean-Paul Sartre, voiced questions about Jewish history that today's generation may answer. Is Judaism the religion of the powerless? Would an empowered community manifest the same empathy and justice for the oppressed? Would an ethic formed in the absence of power instruct a powerful polity? Sartre asked whether the antisemite made the Jew.

American Jewry is now in its fifth generation. The massive immigrations that began in 1881 changed the composition of the community from a small Sephardic and German settlement into a much larger Jewish population, primarily of Eastern European origin. A century later, American Jews are no longer immigrants or the children of immigrants. Distant from the ethnic neighborhoods that constituted what Irving Howe termed "the world of our fathers," these Jews are decades removed from the problems of assimilation, acculturation, and poverty that characterized immigrant life.

American Jews must now write their own story. For five generations, the tale that was told about Jewish existence was vicarious. Jews were Jewish because of what happened to someone else. Jewish life was lived through others, for others. The immigrant generation traced their Jewishness to the European experience, the communities they left behind, their parents and grandparents who remained in the Old World while they journeyed to the New. America was considered a *treife* land, an unholy place. Authentic Judaism was elsewhere.

The children of immigrants were infatuated with America; they abandoned the ethnic neighborhoods and entered the larger society. The Jewish stories they told were of a world left behind: New York's Lower East Side, Boston's Blue Hills Avenue, Philadelphia's Tasker Street, Chicago's West Side.

The next generation moved to the suburbs and maintained a professionalized Judaism, which was the responsibility of paid personnel – rabbis and cantors – but not the province of the folk. Judaism was practiced for one's parents and children. If tradition had a place in the lives of most adults, hired officials were expected to perform it, to observe and transmit the rituals without making excessive demands on congregants.

In recent years, Jewish identity in America has been linked with the Holocaust and Israel. No story that American Jews tell about being Jewish can avoid the awesome defeat of the Holocaust and the rebirth of the State of Israel. However, the overwhelming majority of American Jews are neither survivors nor the children of survivors, and all American Jews have chosen not to be Israelis. Israel – and full participation in the drama of the Jewish state – is but a plane ride away, yet, by definition, American Jews go to Israel as pilgrims, not settlers. For every Jew who moves to Israel to fulfill the Zionist dream, four or five come to America. So even now, American Jews tell a story – important as it may be – that is not theirs although it forms the core of their identity.

My generation was born after the Holocaust. We grew up in a world in which the dream of Israel was a reality – sometimes exhilarating, sometimes mundane, seldom disconcerting or depressing. We came to maturity at a critical moment: during the Six Day War. For three weeks before June 6, 1967, we feared that the Holocaust was about to be repeated. One generation by fire, the next by water; we believed the threat that the Arabs would drive Israel into the sea. Abandoned by the world, the Jews were alone again. And then, we witnessed an unexpected triumph. Syria, Egypt, and Jordan were defeated. After two millennia, Jerusalem was reunited under Jewish rule. Secular Jews were as moved by the seemingly miraculous victory as were their more pious counterparts. All Jews felt joined with the destiny of Israel. Two events were linked by the war: the Holocaust and Israel. The sense of Israeli vulnerability and the possibility of loss touched a deep chord in American Jewry.

The theological works that were written shortly after the 1967 War, and even after the Yom Kippur War six years later, told a simple story about destruction and rebirth, about the ashes of Auschwitz and the stones of Jerusalem. For Richard Rubenstein, Jews had undergone a revolution and reentered history. As they returned to their land their religious consciousness would soon be transformed, paganized – tied to the cycles of mother earth. The God of history was dead, according to Rubenstein, and would be replaced by the God of nature. Jews would become normal people, ordinary rather than central to the divine–human drama. For Emil Fackenheim, the "Commanding Voice of Auschwitz" had been heard, prohibiting posthumous victories for Hitler. Survival itself became a sanctified act. For Eliezer Berkovits, Israel remained pure, aloof from power history in a world of cynicism. Berkovits was convinced that because of its innocence, Israel was again rejected by the world. For Irving Greenberg, Israel was testimony to life, a counterwitness to the death and destruction that Jews suffered in Treblinka and Belzec.

For my generation, the story is more complicated, the reality more problematic. The war in Israel that shaped our adult consciousness was the debacle of Lebanon, followed by the Pollard affair and the Palestinian uprisings. Our tale is more anguished, less innocent, for now the Jewish people are divided, uncertain about the direction of their future.

The essays in this work explore many facets of Jewish existence in America and Israel – religious, political, social, and philosophical. Different chapters represent my efforts to piece together dimensions of the Jewish story – for myself and others. Some sections stand in tension with one another, drawing mutual strength even as they present opposite sides of an issue.

These essays were first drafted for different audiences concerned with the modern Jewish ethos. Some were written for academic conferences and international assemblies, such as the chapter on "The Uniqueness and Universality of the Holocaust" (portions of which were presented at a conference on Operation Reinhard, held in the summer of 1987 at the University of Lublin, and at the Conference on Non-Jewish Victims of Nazi Persecution held at the State Department in February 1987). "Political Zionism's Would-Be Successors" was prepared for a conference on Religion and Politics in the Contemporary World sponsored by the Institute for Values in Public Policy in Washington, D.C. Chapter 1, on "The Nativization of the Holocaust," was delivered to Jewish intellectuals from North America, Israel, and Europe at a conference in Switzerland devoted to Jewish Identity in the Twentieth Century. "Issues in Teaching the Holocaust" was presented to the American Academy of Religion as part of a consultation on the Holocaust and Higher Education.

Several chapters were commissioned by scholarly publications. "The Problem of Pluralism in Contemporary Orthodoxy" was written for a book on American Orthodoxy celebrating the jubilee anniversary of Ramaz School, one of the most liberal Orthodox day schools in America. Portions of the chapters on Elie Wiesel and Jacob Neusner were first drafted for journals requesting reflective essays on the careers of the 1986 Nobel peace prize recipient and one of the most productive Jewish academics in America. Two dialogues have also been included in this collection – because theological reflection not only is the product of scholars talking with scholars but is often the creative interaction among scholars, clergy, and laity wrestling with significant issues. Out of the clashes of opinion, refined for popular audiences, insights are clarified and communicated to nonprofessionals interested in Judaism.

Several chapters reflect the personal experience of this author as a teacher and father and a director of the President's Commission on the Holocaust (now the United States Holocaust Memorial Council). Chapter 3, on the politics of "Public Commemoration of the Holocaust," was written in response to a controversy among Holocaust survivors and other Jews about the diffusion of Holocaust awareness. Several chapters were originally presented to my students at Wesleyan and then Georgetown universities and to a seminar at Yale. At Georgetown, many of my students are deeply rooted in their Roman Catholic faith and trained by a theological faculty of Jesuits, yet they have generously contributed to the theology of a Jewish thinker, himself the product of a parochial education.

Although the origins of the essays are diverse, I have reworked and reframed them as an organic whole. I would like to thank the editors of *Judaism, Sh'ma, The World and I, The Reconstructionist, National Jewish Monthly,* and *Response* for permission to publish and rework material that first appeared in their journals. I am deeply grateful to my wife, Professor Linda Bayer, whose fine hand and sharp pen made this work so much better. She is uncompromising in her search for the precise word and consistent in her demand that I mean what I say and say what I mean. My colleague, friend, teacher, and mentor, Richard L. Rubenstein, has graced this work with a foreword. This book is dedicated in memory of my father, who died but a month shy of his eightieth birthday, after this work was completed but before its publication, and in honor of my mother. She is now four-score years. They have bequeathed me a story and a situation, memories, love, and tradition.

Rabbinic sages have commented that there are three stages in the development of tradition: receiving it; making it one's own by adding experience, insight, and wisdom; and then transmitting it to the next generation. Thus, this work is written for my children – my parents' grandchildren – whose lives will be touched by the questions I ask and the answers I find – or fail to find.

Part I The Holocaust in Contemporary American Culture

1. The Nativization of the Holocaust

American Jews and Israelis are both traumatized by the Holocaust, yet in confronting the same event, these communities draw different conclusions. Similar memories have been recounted to teach diverse lessons. If Israelis turn to the Holocaust as proof that the whole world is against them, American Jews reinforce their commitment to pluralism by recalling the atrocities that sprang from intolerance.

The following essay explores the "nativization" of the Holocaust in two countries and the consequent clash between the stories retold on American soil and those that predominate in Israel. In this chapter I examine the legitimate and inappropriate ways in which past recollections are used to justify the present and construct a future.

The Holocaust has become a symbol central to the identity of American Jewry. Public occasions with Jewish content are incomplete without a required reference to the Holocaust, the memory of which is evoked to rally philanthropists and political activists, to challenge complacency, to undermine or fortify the Jewish establishment, to measure impending danger or bolster solidarity. The authority of the Holocaust is invoked as compelling proof for the veracity of a position. Charges that an opponent's view might encourage the repetition of genocide, or grant Hitler a posthumous victory, are the ultimate epithets. Within the American Jewish community, the Holocaust has entered the domain of shared sacredness.

Perhaps a growing consciousness of the Holocaust was inevitable as the memory of the actual event receded and as those with direct memories of the war – or of Jewish life in prewar Eastern Europe – perished in the fullness of years. Only a generation more distant from the immediate catastrophe could dare to approach it. Like Lot's wife, survivors could not afford to look back while fleeing.

At a safer distance, however, the Holocaust cannot be avoided. Few events in Jewish history are as basic or powerful. Few are as instructive. None is as destructive or transformative.

"By the waters of Babylon we sat down and cried as we remembered Zion." The poet laments Jerusalem's destruction in 586 B.C.E. (before the common era). The psalmist began his sentence in Babylon; the place from which an event is recalled inevitably shapes memory.

Our concern is less with the Holocaust itself than with its recall, less with history than metahistory. How does the place in which a tragedy is remembered shape the collective memory? The two great centers of Jewish life – Israel and America – deal differently with the legacy of destruction, which has permeated the folk and civil religion of each society.

To understand the identity of American Jews, one must first address their Americanism. Within the past half century, American Jews have developed an American identity and sought confirmation of their experience – legitimation for their Jewishness – within mainstream American culture. In the 1950s, Will Herberg taught that America had three religious faiths – Catholicism, Protestantism, and Judaism – and because the American experience made room for Judaism, the suburban migration of the first generation of American Jews enhanced rather than destroyed Jewish institutions. Similarly, the ethnic resurgence of the 1960s gave a new affirmation to Jewishness at a time when the religious foundation of Jewish identity was eroding. Black power made assertions of Jewish solidarity more acceptable. Black studies forced the university to make room for Jewish studies, and the flourishing of Jewish studies that followed was possible only because Jewish studies breached its ethnicity to become nonparochial and secular.[1]

In the seven years between the Six Day War and the Yom Kippur War, the Holocaust became a central part of Jewish consciousness. In the years since, there has also been a determined effort to transmit this traumatic Jewish experience to the American people as a whole and thus enhance its importance to American Jews.

Predictably, the results have been dialectical. To confirm the Holocaust as a major Jewish experience – worthy of its role within

Jewish consciousness – required that it attain recognition within American culture. Yet the very act of reaching out toward a wider audience transformed the recollection and threatened its Judeo-centricity.

Attempts to introduce the Holocaust into the American experience have accelerated. In 1978, President Jimmy Carter created a Presidential Commission on the Holocaust charged with recommending a national Holocaust memorial. The Commission's origin was political – as is almost every presidential action.[2] Carter and his advisers recognized the importance of the Holocaust to the American Jewish community.[3] The date of Carter's announcement coincided with Prime Minister Menachem Begin's visit to Washington (in the middle of the congressional battle over the proposed sale of F-15 bombers to Saudi Arabia) and followed by less than a fortnight the widely successful TV mini-series on the Holocaust. The president chose a dramatic setting to announce the national memorial. One thousand rabbis were invited to the reception at the White House to honor Israel's thirtieth anniversary and welcome Israel's leader.

The Commission recommended a memorial museum that would retell the story of the Holocaust, a program of educational outreach, and national days of remembrance to be observed across the country and in Washington, D.C., where a national ceremony would feature the president and other leaders. Though composed primarily of Jews, the Commission made the deliberate decision to involve the greater American society. Intuitively, the Commission understood that the role of the Holocaust within Jewish consciousness would be strengthened by secular sancta.[4]

In 1975, there were fewer than a dozen courses on the Holocaust offered in American colleges and universities, yet by 1985 the Holocaust was the second most widely taught course of Judaic content – exceeded only by courses in the Hebrew Bible. The Holocaust is also taught in secondary schools throughout the country. Television programs have proliferated; Gerald Green's *Holocaust* was followed by the mini-series on Raoul Wallenberg, John Hersey's *The Wall,* Fania Fenelon's *Playing for Time,* and Richard Rashke's *Escape from Sobibor.* All these broadcasts attracted major audiences and served as important, if flawed, vehicles for educating the American public. In the process, however, the memory and its message changed.

The Holocaust in Israel's Civil Religion

The Holocaust has played a changing role in the civil religion of Israel as the demographic, political, and security conditions of the state have evolved. Charles Liebman and Eliezer Don-Yehiya have argued that Israel's relationship to the Holocaust can be divided into three periods: 1948 to the Eichmann trial; the Eichmann trial to the Yom Kippur War; and the Yom Kippur War to the War in Lebanon.[5] In the aftermath of Lebanon and the Palestinian uprising, Israel will certainly undergo yet another transition with respect to its understanding of the Holocaust.

For the first thirteen years after Israel's establishment as a state, Israeli leaders looked back on the Holocaust with fear and trembling – and with disdain. The only usable past – the only history of that period on which they could base their future – was the heroic chapter of resistance. The fight for Jerusalem or the Negev came to be seen as an extension of the Warsaw Ghetto Uprising. Historians sought to recapture a tradition of resistance defined as armed struggle against an enemy whose goal was genocide. Through oral histories and interviews, Israeli scholars successfully preserved the remnant of that history, not only in Warsaw but in other ghettos, forests, and even the death camps. Jews are fighters, was the lesson. Given only the means, Jews have the will to exact a high price in men and material from the enemy.[6] The new Israeli heroes are not diaspora leaders – neither *stadlanim* (influential intercessors with gentile authorities) nor collaborators – but the proud representatives of a strong, independent people – so went the story.

However, with the Eichmann trial a native Israeli generation was forced to confront on a daily basis the twelve-year odyssey of Jewish extermination that was far more a tale of victimization than heroism. Attorney General Gideon Hausner began the Eichmann trial by invoking Pharaoh, by reviewing three millennia of antisemitism, persecution, and pogroms, which culminated in the Holocaust.[7] The message was unequivocal: There could be no return to the lands of dispersion. Only a sovereign Jewish state could preserve the future.

The Passover *Haggadah* reads: "In every generation they rise against us to extinguish us." The traditional story continues, "but the Holy One, Blessed Be He, saves us from their hands." However, in the absence of a saving God, Israeli Jews turned to human means in order to protect themselves.

The perilous condition of Israel during the Yom Kippur War came as a rude psychological blow to the Israeli national élan. For seventy-two hours, the fate of Israel was dependent on gentile rulers – on an American president whose support for Israel was not matched by his love of Jews (Richard Nixon); on an American secretary of defense who converted from Judaism while a college student at Harvard (James Schlesinger); and on the first secretary of state of the United States who was, to use his own words, "of Jewish origin" (Henry Kissinger).[8] An independent people was humbled to discover themselves dependent on the goodwill of others in order to survive. Almost immediately within Israel, a new understanding developed of the desperate condition of Jews during the Holocaust coupled with furious determination not to return to that condition.

Menachem Begin built upon this realization and constructed a usable past upon the twin pillars of antisemitism and the need for power. *Goyim* (literally, "the nations") hate Jews, Begin maintained. In traditional language, Esau hates Jacob. According to Begin's worldview, Jews are a people that dwells alone. Power is essential. Powerlessness invites victimization. Jews must determine their own morality. The world's pronouncements toward the Jews mask – sometimes more successfully and sometimes less so – their genocidal intent. The desire to make the world *Judenrein* continues, and only fools would allow themselves to be deceived.

In the aftermath of Lebanon and its miscalculations – triggered in part by an inability to separate the politics of the 1980s from the conditions of the 1940s[9] – and with Israel's current economic dependence on the United States, a new historical perspective can be anticipated. Israel's experience as the rulers over hostile and rebellious Palestinians may also reshape the questions Israel asks of the past; its responses may be more complex and more confused.

Meir Kahane's unbridled hatred of the Arabs offers one reading of how Israel may grapple with the memory of the Holocaust. He copies the Nazis and echoes their myths. He longs for one nation, one folk. He wants to expel the alien and make Israel *Arabrein*. Yet, however pernicious Kahane's solution, in contrast to Hitler, Kahane is a great humanitarian because he advocates expulsion with compensation – a far cry from Hitler's Final Solution.[10] The apocalyptic messianism of Gush Emunim offers a second option that threatens to overwhelm Labor's more secular reading of history.[11]

In short, Israel has retold the Holocaust story to mold and reinforce its national saga as it has developed over the past four decades.

The Americanization of the Holocaust

In America, a different reading of the Holocaust has evolved. Two examples may prove instructive. In 1983 the American Gathering of Jewish Holocaust Survivors brought more than 20,000 people to Washington for a three-day conference – the largest single sustained assembly in American Jewish history. The Gathering was convened on the fortieth anniversary of the Warsaw Ghetto Uprising to counteract the widespread and painful perception that Jews went compliantly to their deaths – like sheep to the slaughter – and to give new meaning to the word "resistance": redefined as armed and spiritual. The organizers also wanted to express their commitment to Israel and share their experiences with the American people.

This was not the first gathering of Jewish Holocaust survivors. Two years earlier, 5,000 people from fourteen different countries came to Jerusalem. Amid the sacred shrines of old and new Jerusalem – the Western Wall, Yad Vashem (Israel's national memorial to the Holocaust), and the Knesset building as well as the Warsaw Ghetto Fighters' Kibbutz and Yad Mordecai (a kibbutz near Gaza named after the leader of the Warsaw Ghetto Resistance, Mordecai

Anielewicz) – survivors assembled and formally transmitted their legacy to the next generation.[12]

When meeting in Washington, by contrast, the survivors were surrounded by other national shrines – the Capitol, the White House, the Washington Monument, Arlington Cemetery, the Lincoln and Vietnam memorials. Much to the surprise of the survivors themselves, America became the dominant theme of the conference – or at least the survivors' unique sense of America.

There were expressions of pride and appreciation for America, the land of opportunity and liberty. "Our adopted country has been kind to us," said one survivor from Poland, "and we in turn have contributed in some small way to build a strong and just society based on equality and justice for all." Another survivor said, "America embraced us when we felt rejected. America gave us the feeling of belonging when we were stateless." There were words of gratitude to America for defeating the Nazis, liberating the concentration camps, welcoming survivors, supporting Israel, and establishing a national Holocaust memorial.

Of course, there were also words of bitterness and sadness as survivors recalled long lines at U.S. consulates, quotas restricting refugees, ships turned away from American shores, gates closed to fleeing Jews, and bombs dropped everywhere but at Auschwitz. Unlike earlier immigrant generations, survivors are a reminder not only of the American dream but of America's failure to serve as a haven in the hour of greatest need.[13]

During the three-day gathering in Washington, some survivors spoke of themselves as the embodiment of the American dream. Driven from their native lands by a tyrant, they came to America bereft of material possessions but fueled by a love of freedom. Through industry and initiative, they rebuilt their lives, raised children and grandchildren, and became an integral part of American life – adding to the rich mosaic of American culture their unique heritage of *Yiddishkeit* and *Menschlichkeit* (humaneness). They portrayed themselves as incarnations of the simple values that are the essence of the American experience – courage and dignity, hope and defiance.

When survivors gathered in Jerusalem, they came as pilgrims to add their experience to the Jewish national saga, to which they felt inextricably connected. When they came to Washington, they offered their experience as part of the American drama, to which they also belonged.

A second example of Americanization of the Holocaust has occurred in high school classrooms. In 1979–81, a team of educational researchers, psychologists, historians, and sociologists worked on a study of four different Holocaust curricula – material developed by teachers and students in Great Neck, New York; Brookline, Massachusetts; Philadelphia, Pennsylvania; and New York City, along with the written curricula of several other cities. [14]

In the early 1980s, a debate concerning the Holocaust's comprehensibility dominated the theological literature on the Holocaust. Theologically, the Holocaust appeared as the *mysterium tremendum* – the awesome mystery – which cannot be penetrated. This insight forms the core of Emil Fackenheim's theological work and was the basis of Elie Wiesel's "Plea for the Survivors." Wiesel argued that the nonsurvivor can only approach the gates of the event and view it indistinctly from afar.

The Holocaust Memorial Council was engaged in a long and bitter debate concerning the uniqueness and universality of the Holocaust. Was the Holocaust an unprecedented event – a universe apart from the experience of the Armenians under Turkish rule, the slaughter in Biafra, the auto-genocide of Cambodia, and the suffering of non-Jewish nationals under Nazi occupation in Eastern Europe? Were Jews the only victims of the Holocaust? How should the Holocaust be defined?

Simon Wiesenthal suggested a universalist definition that was adopted by President Carter in the formal documents of the Commission and its successor body, the United States Holocaust Memorial Council: "The Holocaust is the destruction of six million Jews and five million non-Jews by the Nazis and their collaborators during World War II. [15] Yehuda Bauer, the distinguished Israeli historian, attacked the Carter–Wiesenthal definition. He argued that the Holocaust was the systematic, state-sponsored extermination of 6 million Jews as an intentional act of state undertaken in pursuit of what the Nazis considered a redemptive goal.[16] Wiesel sought language that would protect the uniqueness of the Holocaust and differentiate between the Jewish and non-Jewish victims of Nazism. The Holocaust, he argued, "was the systematic, bureaucratic extermination of six million Jews by the Nazis and their collaborators as a central act of state during the Second World War; as night descended, millions of other people were swept into this net of death."[17] "While not all the victims were Jews," Wiesel wrote, "all Jews were victims." In this way, Wiesel negotiated the labyrinth between those who argued for a Judeo-centric uniqueness and the requirement of universality imposed by the president.

To Jews in Israel and in America, the Holocaust was a source of distinctiveness, albeit a horrible one, among peoples. Jews were different, a nation set apart – chosen, if not by the God of Israel, then at least by the enemies of that God.[18] Christianity had provided the Nazis with the choice of the Jew as victim, and Christian teaching and institutions did not have the moral force to resist Nazism. Modernity had also failed. The political, economic, bureaucratic, and demographic trends of modern Western society set the stage for the Holocaust. If a scientifically developed, culturally advanced, and philosophically sophisticated Germany could perpetrate the Holocaust, then the West itself had failed.

While theologians and politicians debated the universality and comprehensibility of the Holocaust, teachers and students were able to understand both the uniqueness of the Holocaust and its universality. In numerous public school systems studied by Mary Glynn and Geoffrey Bock in their work *American Youth and the Holocaust,* instruction in the Holocaust had become an instrument for teaching the professed values of American society: democracy, pluralism, respect for differences, individual responsibility, freedom from prejudice, and an abhorrence of racism. High school students of the Holocaust and their teachers were essentially uninterested in the debate that consumed theologians and historians. They viewed the Holocaust as an extreme example of what could happen if the core values of American society were consistently abrogated. All the curricula Glynn and Bock studied had a common methodological assumption, which negated mystery. They saw the Holocaust as a human experience – committed and endured by human beings. As such, the Holocaust can be discussed and even understood by students in grades seven through twelve.

Holocaust curricula were not used, as some had feared, to differentiate between Jews and non-Jews. Instead, they became a means of reducing barriers between students. One black student spoke of telling the story of the Holocaust in his Brooklyn neighborhood and getting the following response: "God, we thought *we* had it bad." In Great Neck, with its large Jewish population, a study of the Holocaust reportedly sparked some of the most honest and personal discussions the students had ever had.

The question of "universalizing" the Holocaust (of comparing it to other events or removing it from an exclusively or predominantly Jewish context) pitted Jews against non-Jews in literary journals. In his book *A Double Dying,* Alvin Rosenfeld wrote:

> *Sophie's Choice . . .* is another prominent example of the tendency to universalize Auschwitz as a murderous thrust against mankind. As such, it has the effect, and no doubt the intention, of removing the Holocaust from its place within Jewish and Christian history and placing it within the generalized history of evil, for which no one in particular need be held accountable.[19]

Rosenfeld objected to William Styron's tendency – shared by other American writers and by the teachers interviewed in the study of Holocaust curriculum – to view the Holocaust from the perspective of his own experience; Styron and others place the Holocaust in categories alien to the event but native to American soil. In Styron's case, Stingo's encounter with the Holocaust was shaped by his early experience of racism, domination, and violence – that is, by his personal history as a sensitive Southerner growing up during the war. Styron chose Richard Rubenstein's *The Cunning of History* as his text because it approached the Holocaust from a perspective he understood; Rubenstein described the Holocaust as an expression of human slavery in the extreme – and thus in continuity with *The Confessions of Nat Turner.*

Norbert Samuelson has suggested that the cultural debate may be both personal and ideological. Elie Wiesel's passion, sentimentality, and fervor have shaped American Jewry's image of the Holocaust. Arthur Miller's television script *Playing for Time* created a character with which the secular Jewish left can identify. William Styron appropriates the Holocaust for gentiles, and Eliezer Berkovits's work *With God in Hell* reclaims the Holocaust for pious Jewish believers.

As the study of the Holocaust passes out of the ghetto and into the mainstream of American culture, it will inevitably be reunderstood in different categories – and thus, in part, dejudaized. In American high schools, as in Styron's work, the Holocaust was not "generalized" (not, for example, viewed as just another act of violence undifferentiated from all others); rather, it was regarded as distinct – unique because its scale and content were unprecedented – even though it was analyzed within a secular context.

The authors of the curricula study concluded:

> As an event of this magnitude is incorporated into the American educational system, the lens through which the data is seen is necessarily an American one. The categories relate to the experience of American students throughout the country and also to their teachers. There is no way of resisting this tide, and indeed from our research, we find that the uniqueness of the Holocaust is underscored by this process of filtration and absorption. Indeed, its specialness is its own best witness, communicating itself most profoundly, most clearly and incontrovertibly.[20]

Optimism and the Reality of Auschwitz

Americans tend to be optimistic; the national ethos avoids the tragic or searches for a silver lining behind dark clouds. This hopeful tendency has reflected itself in the ways Americans deal with the Holocaust intellectually. Popularizers of the Holocaust have tended to look for cheap grace, for easy sources of consolation. They have sought to minimize evil or severely limit its implications.

Some writers have focused on the righteous gentile as a source of hope. Three cases come readily to mind: one a country, the second a village, and the third an individual – Denmark, Le Chambon, and Raoul Wallenberg. Each case is powerfully consoling, each simple in its common humanity. And each has entered the domain of legend.

Denmark saved 92 percent of its Jews. When questioned, however, the Danes explain that they did nothing extraordinary; they simply treated Jews as fellow citizens facing persecution from an oppressive occupying army. The villagers of Le Chambon were raised on a tradition of hospice; Protestants in Catholic France – themselves persecuted – they just did what they had been taught to do when young Jewish children came knocking at their doors. Wallenberg was frustrated sitting on the sidelines while the action was taking place elsewhere; he couldn't side with the despised Nazis, nor could he continue diplomatic business as usual.

No matter how touching these examples of humanity and heroism, righteous gentiles were numerically rare. There was an extraordinary imbalance between their accomplishment – however noble and glorious – and the victims' needs. As we look at the landscape of Europe, complicity and cowardice were the norm. Indifference was widespread. This reality does not demean the deeds of the few, but the flicker of hope that these exceptions generated is overwhelmed by darkness. Instead of pointing to religious heroes and martyrs – a Dietrich Bonhoeffer, an André Trochmé, or a Martin Niemoller – Christians must confront the uncomfortable fact that church teaching allowed the Jews to be chosen as victims.

Religious practice measurably influenced the behavior of the perpetrators and the response of the bystanders. There was a direct correlation between the intensity of religious practice and the percentage of Jews killed in an occupied territory. Where Christians were most devout – in Poland, Slovakia, and the Baltic countries – the percentage of Jews killed increased (90% in Poland, 89% in Slovakia, 90% in the Baltic states of Latvia, Lithuania, and Estonia).[21]

President Ronald Reagan expressed the naive sense of American optimism in his decision to visit Bitburg and in the statements he made at Bitburg and Bergen-Belsen. Reagan sought to narrow the scope of the Holocaust. It was proper, he thought, to pay tribute to German soldiers. They were honorable men who died on the battlefield for a dishonorable cause. Once he discovered that members of the Waffen S.S. were buried at Bitburg, Reagan further narrowed the scope of evil. He claimed that Waffen S.S. were acceptable – after all, many of these men were only teenage conscripts – it was the S.S. elite volunteers, according to Reagan, who were actually to blame for killing Jews.

At Bitburg, Reagan further constricted the dimensions of evil speaking as if Hitler alone had been responsible for the Holocaust. According to his speech, the entire apparatus of destruction rested on the shoulders of one man as good people were led astray. Reagan conveniently overlooked the assistance that the German military gave the S.S. Einsatzgruppen on the Russian front, not to mention the pervasiveness of Nazism within German society and the role of the S.S. in Western Europe. Not to be confused by facts, Reagan minimized, personalized, and limited the evil of the Holocaust.

America's optimistic tendencies are also reflected in a more sophisticated and serious way by the late Terrance Des Pres in *The Survivor: An Anatomy of Life in the Death Camps.* In this moving study of Holocaust survivors – and survivors of the Soviet Gulag – Des Pres poignantly describes the victims' suffering and their struggle. He does not hesitate to detail graphically the survivors' anguish. Neither does he shy away from the unseemly – ruthlessness, aggressiveness, sexuality, and excremental assault. Yet in his final chapter on "Radical Nakedness" – at the lowest point of despair in the book – Des Pres detects what he terms the essence of human survival. Quoting a survivor, he states: "It wasn't the ruthlessness that enabled an individual to survive – it was an intangible quality, not particular to educated or sophisticated individuals . . . . It is best described as an overriding thirst – perhaps, too, a talent for life, and a faith in life."[22]

Des Pres concludes:

> Much of the behavior of survivors may thus be traced to the "biosocial" roots of human existence; and not their behavior merely, but also the extraordinary stubbornness of will which characterizes action in extremity – the furious energy of a will impersonal and stronger than hope, which in an accurate, unmetaphorical sense can only be that of life itself.[23]

One cannot fail to be touched by the power of Des Pres's words and awesome experience he describes. Yet, as Lawrence Langer has argued, "from the perspective of the victims, who far out-number the survivors, the disorder of meaningless death contra-dicts the ordering impulses of time. Those who died for nothing in the Holocaust left the living with a paralyzing dilemma of fac-ing a perpetually present grief."[24]

As an event, the Holocaust cannot be reduced to order, to a system for survival, or even to a sense of overriding meaning. The Holocaust defies meaning and negates hope. The scope of victimization reduces even survival to a nullity. The reality of Auschwitz should silence optimists.

Some may argue that the nativization of the Holocaust distorts the event. The Holocaust took place on the soil of Europe and to the body of the Jewish people. But only a part of memory in-volves the past. The past image is projected on a screen of the present with which it interacts, and this new image in turn sheds light on the future. In addressing the authenticity of memory, we must examine both its source and its projection.

History reconstitutes itself in memory. Although American and Israeli Jews remember the same event as basic to their identity, and even though the memory of that event cements the link be-tween them, the present reality and national sagas of these two communities are so different that what is gleaned from the past for the future may increasingly diverge.

The tide of Americanization cannot easily be avoided because in order for Israeli scholarship to move beyond its shores, it must reach out to its Western brethren. For Jews to solidify the place of the Holocaust within Jewish consciousness, they must establish its importance for the American people as a whole. The process can-not be reversed for the decision has already been made. By sharing a private and painful experience with the world, Jews have trans-formed it; in turn, it has changed us.

2. The Uniqueness and Universality of the Holocaust

For more than a decade the debate over the uniqueness and universality of the Holocaust has divided scholars, survivors, and civic leaders on three continents. Israeli historians have vehemently opposed the representation of non-Jewish victims in the U.S. Holocaust Memorial Museum, fearing that this inclusion diminishes the singularity of Jewish fate. In this chapter, I argue that only by discusssing all of the Nazi's victims can the uniqueness of Jewish suffering be convincingly conveyed as a matter of fact rather than a statement of faith. When uniqueness is irrefutable, analogies need not be feared since they cannot be mistaken for equivalents.

Because the Shoah *is a novum in Jewish history, an unprecedented event, it has revolutionized faith and politics.*

The question of the uniqueness and universality of the Holocaust is being considered with increasing frequency not only in scholarly quarters with a focus on historiography but also in communities throughout the United States where Holocaust memorials and commemorative services raise a consciousness of the Holocaust, which then enters the mainstream of American culture. In the process the word "Holocaust," shorn of its particular reference along with its article, threatens to become a symbolic word connoting mass murder and destruction whatever the magnitude. The debate over the place of the Holocaust in history is being conducted within the academy, in the streets among ethnic politicians and community leaders, in schools by educators developing curricula, among a cultural elite in literature and the arts, and in religious and philosophical circles.

Perhaps the force of personality, as much as circumstance, has brought the definition of the Holocaust to the fore. The chief protagonists for alternate conceptions, Elie Wiesel and Simon Wiesenthal, are both survivors, both European Jews, both men of towering stature who have brought the Holocaust to the world's attention. Yet these two men differ markedly in their personal histories, their legacy and destiny. Simon Wiesenthal defines the word "Holocaust" as the systematic murder of 11 million people, of whom 6 million were Jews killed because of their Jewishness, and 5 million were non-Jews – Gypsies, Jehovah's Witnesses, homosexuals, political prisoners, Poles, Ukrainians, the handicapped and the mentally ill – killed for a variety of reasons in an apparatus of destruction designed for mass extermination. The machinery of destruction included the Einsatzgruppen, the concentration camps, and the extermination camps with their gas chambers and ovens. Wiesenthal maintains that although all Jews were victims, the Holocaust transcended the confines of the Jewish community. Other people shared the tragic fate of victimhood.

Wiesenthal personifies two traditional self-characterizations of the Jewish people, *din* (justice) and *am kisheh oref* (a stiff-necked people); he has been tenacious in his pursuit of law, demanding that the European nations bring their Nazi war criminals to trial. He has stubbornly refused to abandon the quest for justice after some forty-five years, even when its meaning may have been tarnished by international disinterest and by the absence of appropriately severe sentences. (One war criminal was recently sentenced to the equivalent of one and a half *minutes* in jail for every person he killed.) Wiesenthal has resisted the temptation to revenge – a swifter, more primitive form of punishment. He hounds both the criminal and the state to reaffirm the value of justice.

Wiesenthal's inclusion of non-Jewish victims enhances his basic post-Holocaust commitment, the prosecution of Nazi war criminals. When apathetic governments are reminded that their non-Jewish citizens were also killed, a greater measure of cooperation can be enlisted. By more broadly defining the Holocaust, Wiesenthal can intensify the political pressure he exerts. Wiesenthal's more universal predilection may also reflect his present status as a European Jew; he belongs to a demoralized community that may be psychologically incapable of taking a Judeo-centric perspective in the public domain, preferring instead the aphorism of Judah Leib Gordon to "be a Jew in your own home and a man in the street."[1] Wiesenthal's statements regarding Kurt Waldheim's Nazi past similarly indicate the limits of his situation as an Austrian Jew.

Wiesenthal feared the resurgence of Austrian antisemitism and was reluctant to press the Waldheim matter. He also failed to take the lead in challenging President Reagan's visit to Bitburg. (The Los Angeles Center for Holocaust Studies that bears Wiesenthal's name is led by more secure American-born Orthodox Jews who were less inhibited in exposing Waldheim's past and decrying Bitburg.)

Wiesenthal's insistence that the non-Jew was also a victim of the Holocaust mirrors his experience in Mauthausen, where Jews constituted only a minority of those incarcerated. Unlike Wiesel, who was deported and incarcerated almost exclusively with Jews, Wiesenthal spent the war years in an integrated environment.

Nevertheless, it should be noted that among two hundred panels on display in the Simon Wiesenthal Center (as of 1988), fewer than 7 percent deal with non-Jews, and half of these displays concern righteous individuals who lived and fought with Jews or helped rescue Jews. Critics who would contend that the Wiesenthal Center dilutes the Jewish meaning of the Holocaust had better look elsewhere for the substantiation of their accusations.

Wiesenthal is not the only person who has included non-Jews among Holocaust victims, nor has he become an active participant in the debate over definition. Rather, his general position in the past has led others to perceive his stance in universalist terms that some interpret as an affront to the unique experience of the Jews in the Holocaust.

By contrast, Elie Wiesel is regarded as the poet laureate of the Holocaust, a man who has become – in the words of Steven Schwarzschild – "the defacto high priest of our generation, the one who speaks most tellingly in our time of our hopes and fears, our tragedy and our protest."[2] For Wiesel the Holocaust is a sacred mystery that can be approached but never understood; the Holocaust is the modern *Pardes,* a world that can be apprehended only at great peril and that should not be studied without preparation and caution. Elsewhere I have written at length of Wiesel's significance as a thinker and his impact on contemporary Jewish consciousness.[3] Wiesel is invaluable as a storyteller who has passionately conveyed the memory of the Holocaust.

Wiesel fears that Wiesenthal's definition of the Holocaust may trigger an irreversible process that will erase the memory of 6 million Jews. He contends that people will speak first of 11 million people, 6 million of whom were Jews; then of 11 million people, some of whom were Jews; and finally of 11 million people, deleting any reference to Jews.[4]

Wiesel is the only major American Jewish novelist who writes solely from a Jewish perspective and for whom the process of Americanization was peripheral to his personal story and literary contribution. Even though Wiesel has been an American citizen for three decades and was twice honored with medals by his country, he continues to write in French and sets most of his novels in Europe and Israel; few American characters even appear. (*Day,* a rare exception, is set in New York but deals with the psychological scars left by the Holocaust on a survivor, thus rendering the American setting irrelevant. *The Fifth Son* begins in America but quickly moves to Europe.) Nevertheless, it was as an American figure that Wiesel was appointed chairman of the President's Commission on the Holocaust and its successor body, the United States Holocaust Memorial Council. These public bodies were created to transmit the legacy of Jewish suffering to a general American audience.

The task of the U.S. Holocaust Memorial Council involved the Americanization of the Holocaust; the story had to be told in such a way that it would resonate not only with the survivor in New York and his children in Houston or San Francisco, but with a black leader from Atlanta, a midwestern farmer, or a northeastern industrialist. Millions of Americans make pilgrimages to Washington; the Holocaust Museum must take them back in time, transport them to another continent, and inform their current reality. The Americanization of the Holocaust is an honorable task provided that the story told is faithful to the historical event. Each culture inevitably leaves its stamp on the past it remembers. The intersection of historical event and social need, what happened and what can be understood, leaves neither history nor society unchanged. This process is integral to what sociologists term the "civil religion" of a given society.

Designing a Holocaust Museum in America will be far more difficult than planning Yad Vashem in Israel because the United States Holocaust Memorial Museum must address an audience that finds the tale itself alien. The American museum also runs the risk of creating a magnet for antisemitism if others who perceive themselves, rightly or wrongly, as victims of the Holocaust feel excluded from the memorial or sense that their suffering has been trivialized or denied. The museum must grapple with the problem of complicity with the Nazis in the destruction of the Jews by people who were themselves the victims of Nazism. The American Holocaust Museum must also explore the dilemma of the bystander in a way that makes sense of the few successes and many failures of American policy regarding the Holocaust during and following the war. Because this museum is a government project (appointments to the Council are made by the president), the Council cannot be fully insulated from the political context in which it operates.

Yehuda Bauer, the prominent historian and head of the Institute of Contemporary Jewry at the Hebrew University in Jerusalem, voiced the fear that historical truths would be sacrificed for political expediency in the American Council's work. Bauer noted two definitions of the Holocaust offered in speeches by President Jimmy Carter. Carter spoke of a memorial to "six million Jews and millions of other victims of Nazism during World War II." On another occasion he decried the "systematic and state-sponsored extermination of 6 million Jews and 5 million non-Jews." Bauer comments: "The memorial as seen by the President [not the commission] should commemorate all the victims of Nazism, Jews and non-Jews *alike* and should *submerge* the specific Jewish tragedy in the general sea of atrocities committed by the Nazi regime."[5]

Bauer attributed the "submersion" of the specific Jewish tragedy to pressure from American ethnic groups and warned that an Americanized, non-Jewish memorial would misrepresent the Holocaust.

Bauer marshaled three highly emotional arguments to foster his claim. He invoked the Soviet attempt to deny the Jewishness of the Holocaust, which resulted in the abominable memorial at Babi Yar where no mention of Jews is made in either the content of the sculpture or the inscription on the memorial. Second, Bauer referred to the Western denial of the "War Against the Jews," which led to the failure to rescue. Third, Bauer alluded to international antisemitism, which seeks to deny the Holocaust altogether.

We must separate the emotional elements of these arguments from their substantive components. Ironically, Bauer focuses on Carter when the responsibility for designing and implementing the museum has been delegated to the Holocaust Memorial Council, which consistently emphasized the uniqueness of the Jewish experience.

Bauer gave undue importance to a president's words on a ceremonial occasion while neglecting the deliberations of the Presidential Commission and its *Report to the President* along with the actual work of the Council. Furthermore, Bauer mistook the intention to "include" others (non-Jews) in the museum for a total "submergence" of Jewish suffering in a "sea of atrocities." In fact, the uniqueness of the Jewish experience can best be documented by comparing it with the Nazi treatment of other persecuted populations. Only by understanding the fate of other groups, detailing where it paralleled Jewish treatment and, more importantly, where it differed, can the distinctive nature of Jewish fate be historically demonstrated.

With respect to Bauer's fear of Americanization, the question of audience should not be confused with content. The Holocaust is only "Americanized" insofar as it is explained to Americans and related to their history with ramifications for future policy. The study of the Holocaust can provide insights that have universal import for the destiny of all humanity. A national council funded at taxpayers' expense to design a *national* memorial does not have the liberty to create an exclusively Jewish one in the restricted sense of the term, and most specifically with regard to audience. A purely Jewish museum is the task of the American Jewish community operating with private funding and without government subvention, as is the case with the New York Holocaust Memorial (appropriately titled "The Museum of the Jewish Heritage"). In the final analysis, private Jewish memorials and the national Holocaust museum (along with scholarship, art, and media productions) will define the Holocaust for the American public, not the words of an ineloquent president.

Bauer does provide his readers with a valuable definition of the uniqueness of the Holocaust: the planned, total annihilation of an entire community and a quasi-apocalyptic, religious component whereby the death of the victim became an integral ingredient in the drama of salvation. Bauer presents two necessary but not exhaustive conditions for the uniqueness of the Holocaust.

Survivors (and some other Jews as well) have been fundamentally ambivalent about bequeathing the story of the Holocaust. For the Holocaust to have any sustained impact, it must enter the mainstream of international consciousness as a symbolic word denoting a particular, extraordinary event with moral, political, and social implications. Yet the moment it enters the mainstream, the Holocaust becomes fair game for writers, novelists, historians, theologians, and philosophers with different backgrounds and unequal skills. Some lesser minds or insensitive thinkers are bound to disappoint, dilute, and misrepresent.

Transmitting the Holocaust entails a degree of uncontrolled dissemination. Jews cannot simultaneously maintain the Holocaust as a horribly sanctified and inviolate topic while complaining that the world is ignorant of its occurence. Even for Wiesel, the decision to run the risks of exposure began when he published *Night* in French. (The Yiddish original had been published two years earlier in Argentina.)

Uniqueness of Intent or Methodology

Bauer displayed no discomfort with the word "Holocaust" even though the term itself is not without its problems. "Holocaust" is a theological term in origin rather than a historical one. It is an English word derivative from the Greek translation of the Hebrew word *olah,* meaning a sacrificial offering burnt whole before the Lord. The word itself softens and falsifies the Holocaust by imparting religious meaning.[6] The Yiddish word *hurban,* meaning destruction, is starker and refers to the results of the event itself. The Hebrew word *Shoah* shares much in common with its Yiddish antecedent. Bauer locates the uniqueness of the Holocaust in the intentionality of the perpetrators. This view is essentially supported by Lucy Dawidowicz, Uriel Tal, George Mosse, and Steven Katz. These scholars emphasize intent and ideology.

By contrast, Raul Hilberg and other historians have focused on results rather than intentions. Hilberg concentrates not on the philosophy that underscored the destruction but on the processes of execution. Emil Fackenheim, Lawrence Langer, Hannah Arendt,

Richard Rubenstein, and Joseph Borkin concur with this function-alist approach. *How* the terrible crime was committed, as much as its theoretical conception, distinguishes the Holocaust from previous manifestations of evil.

Joseph Borkin has argued that Auschwitz represented the perverse perfection of slavery. In all previous manifestations of human slavery, including the particularly cruel form practiced in North America, slaves were considered a capital investment to be protected, fed, and sheltered by the master. Slaves were permitted to reproduce and hence to increase the master's wealth. By contrast, the Nazis reduced human beings to consumable raw materials expended in the process of manufacture. All mineral life was systematically drained from the bodies, which were recycled into the Nazi war economy; gold teeth went to the treasury, hair was used for mattresses, ashes became fertilizer. At I.G. Auschwitz the average slave lived for ninety days; at Buna, he lived for thirty days. One survivor explained, "they oiled the machines, but they didn't feed the people." These corporate decisions were made in Frankfurt, and *not* in the field, for "sound" economic reasons and not under the exigencies of battlefield conditions.[7]

Beyond the "perfection" of slavery, the elimination of surplus population was also carried to its logical conclusion. Bureaucracy was employed to solve complex problems in implementing mass destruction. The coexistence of demonic evil with banality pervaded the bureaucratic structure.[8] The camps themselves were a society of total domination.

A Lachrymose Theory of Jewish History

Ismar Schorsch, a prominent Jewish historian and now chancellor of the Conservative Jewish Theological Seminary, advocated a limited role for the Holocaust in the civil religion of American Jews. Schorsch feared the development of a lachrymose theory of Jewish history.[9] The history of Jew as victim threatens to dominate Jewish consciousness, to diminish the totality of Jewish history in which Jews were the authors of their own destiny, and to overwhelm the vital celebration of life or the hope for redemption.

In addition, Schorsch argued, the consequence of an overemphasis on the Holocaust has been an "obsession with the uniqueness of the event as if to forgo the claim would be to diminish the horror of the crime."[10]

The truth, Schorsch maintained, is that Jews were the only victims of genocide in World War II. "To insist on more is to imply or overindulge in invidious comparisons." When used indiscriminately, the argument for the uniqueness of the Holocaust is a "throwback to an age of religious polemics, a secular version of chosenness."[11] This misuse of the uniqueness argument to reinforce chosenness is seen most clearly in the writings of the Orthodox Jewish theologian Eliezer Berkovits: "The metaphysical quality of the Nazi-German hatred of the Jews as well as the truly diabolical, superhuman quality of the Nazi-German criminality against the Jews are themselves testimonies to the dark knowledge with which a nazified Germany sensed the presence in history of the hiding God."[12]

For Schorsch, the claim of uniqueness may be true, but it is politically counterproductive because it "impedes dialogue and introduces issues that alienate potential allies from among other victims of organized depravity," that is, other victims of Nazism: Armenians, Gypsies, blacks, and so on. Schorsch recommends that Jews translate their experience into existential and political symbols meaningful to non-Jews without "submerging our credibility."

What for Schorsch is the process of translation appears to Bauer as Americanization and dejudaization. Bauer's characterization of the Holocaust's uniqueness is inadequate (since it is limited to intentionality), and Schorsch's resistance to history is inappropriate. Both Bauer's assertions and Schorsch's reticence could be informed by a more comparative approach. The fruits of such consideration are amply apparent in such important works as Irving Horowitz's study of the Holocaust and the Armenian genocide, *Taking Lives,* Helen Fein's *Accounting for Genocide,* and the literary analysis of Terrence Des Pres. A recognition of uniqueness need not alienate potential allies for it can sharpen insight and encourage research. Nevertheless, Schorsch's inhibiting cautions, like

Bauer's misplaced fears, should be taken as warning signals of what must be avoided in order to secure serious scholarship and its responsible application.

Conferring Status

John Cuddihy of Hunter College is a brilliant yet eccentric critic of contemporary American Jewry. His insights sometimes glisten even if they do not long endure, yet his information is wide-ranging and his understanding of modernity and the Jewish condition is comprehensive and original. Cuddihy probes not the history of the Holocaust but its historiography.[13]

Cuddihy cited a number of scholars, all of whom are making similar points regarding the Holocaust's uniqueness in character and organization, in its systematic and noninstrumental preoccupation with murder, in its totality and its focus on death. Henry Feingold, an important historian of the Roosevelt administration, fears that the Holocaust may be robbed of its "horrendous particularity." People may generalize history and modulate Nazism by treating it not as a uniquely demonic force but as the dark side of the human spirit that lurks in all of us. A. Roy Eckhardt, a Christian theologian of the Holocaust, terms the event "uniquely unique," a category apart from all other historical events. In his critical work *The Cunning of History*, Richard Rubenstein projects the precedent of the Holocaust toward its present and future ramifications, as noted by William Styron both in his introduction to Rubenstein's work and in his novel *Sophie's Choice*. For both Rubenstein and Styron, the Holocaust looms as the ultimate technological nightmare, the manifestation extraordinaire of the potentialities of Western civilization. Emil Fackenheim, by contrast, believes that the uniqueness of the Holocaust is found in the uniqueness of its victims. The Holocaust was directed against Jews who were "not the *waste products* of Nazi society but its *end products*."[14]

In reviewing these claims of uniqueness, Cuddihy has noticed that the distinction between Jews and non-Jews is the key element that unites Fackenheim and Feingold, Bauer and Wiesel. The "residual category" of non-Jews that continues to divide the world serves three critical functions for Jews. It preserves a sense of sacred particularity, freezing the presence of antisemitism in Jewish consciousness and thus preempting the Sartresque question: "Why remain a Jew?" It continues to separate Jew from Gentile not as a free choice by Jews but as a decision imposed by Hitler, who radically divided Jews from non-Jews. Finally, according to Cuddihy, uniqueness functions not so much to prevent historical fraud or dejudaization but as a device for conferring status.

In fairness to Cuddihy, we must stress that his concern is not history but sociology, and he is writing something of a cryptosociology of historiography. Often one can dissent from his views with ease, especially when his statements are flip or inaccurate. Yet one must examine his claim that inherent in the desire to affirm the uniqueness of the Holocaust – apart from the issue of its factual validity – may be a secular translation of Jewish chosenness wherein a people's specialness, once derived spiritually from the divine revelation at Sinai, is now recast as the inheritance of those wronged by the demonic anti-God (so to speak) who acted at Auschwitz.

In response to Cuddihy's critique, we must consider the factual basis for the Holocaust's uniqueness and the resistance to its centrality in contemporary Jewish consciousness.

The Holocaust in Jewish History

The discussion of the uniqueness and universality of the Holocaust in world history is accompanied by queries regarding the place of the Holocaust in Jewish history. The current discussion centers on two major questions: (1) Does the Holocaust occupy an excessively prominent position in contemporary Jewish consciousness, threatening to obscure the promise of Sinai, the triumph of Israel, and the totality of previous Jewish history? (2) Does the Holocaust have normative implications for Jewish history and theology? The parameters of the dialogue have been set by Jacob Neusner, Irving Greenberg, Paula Hyman, Michael Wyschograd, Robert Alter, Arnold Wolf, and myself.[15] Essential to the general argument for the uniqueness of the Holocaust is the conclusion that the Holocaust is not only quantitatively but also qualitatively different from other episodes of persecution in Jewish history, a point not universally accepted by scholars in the field whose objections are often motivated by the politics and aesthetics of Holocaust commemoration rather than by specific historical data.

Another set of objections to the Holocaust's uniqueness comes from religious Jews who seek to minimize the Holocaust's importance in order to limit the damage done to religious faith. These pietists view the Holocaust as another event in the long line of Jewish tales of suffering and woe – less significant, perhaps, than the destruction of the first and second Temples though surely more important than the 1492 expulsion of Jews from Spain or the 1648 Chmielnitski massacres in the Ukraine. After all, these thinkers argue, martyrdom and misery have often been the lot of Jews throughout their long and painful history. After each catastrophe Jewish faith has confronted the suffering, and Jews have remained faithful to the covenant. Most Jews who share this view are believers for whom too much is at stake to permit a fundamental reexamination of faith.

The most significant Jewish critique of the uniqueness argument comes from those thinkers who do not believe that the experience of the Holocaust is adequate to sustain the Jewish future. Michael Wyschograd, a New York–based philosopher who sought refuge in the United States from Germany, writes:

> Israel's faith has always centered on the saving acts of God: the election, the Exodus, the Temple and the Messiah. However more prevalent destruction was in the history of Israel, the acts of destruction were enshrined in minor fast days while those of redemption became the joyous proclamation of Passover and Tabernacles. . . . The God of Israel is a redeeming God; this is the only message we are authorized to proclaim.[16]

However, Wyschograd does not tell us how to speak of a redeeming God in the age of Auschwitz. When truth is sacrificed to expediency, the result is propaganda (however useful psychologically or theologically). It may be traditional to emphasize good over evil, but in the face of overwhelming destruction, this perspective may cease to be credible.

The Holocaust is unprecedented in Jewish history; it was not simply a continuation of traditional antisemitism for four fundamental reasons. The Holocaust differs from previous manifestation of antisemitism in that the earlier expressions were episodic, nonsustained, illegal (they took place outside the law), and religiously rather than biologically based. That is, Jews were killed for what they believed or practiced: Conversion or emigration were possible alternatives. By contrast, the Nazis were unrelenting; for twelve years the destruction of the Jewish people was a German priority. Trains that could have been used to bring soldiers to the front or transport injured personnel to the rear were diverted to bring Jews to their death. The persecution of Jews was geographically widespread throughout Europe from Central Russia to the Spanish border. Furthermore, it was legally conducted, the legal system serving as an instrument of oppression. The persecution of Jews and their annihilation was a policy of state, utilizing all facets of the government. Most importantly, Jews were killed not for *what* they were or for what they practiced or believed, but for the *fact* that they were – all Jews were to be exterminated, not merely the Jewish soul. Jews were no longer considered, as they were in Christian theology, the symbol of evil; rather, they were regarded as subhuman and were thus eliminated.

Even the traditional category of Jewish martyrdom was denied to the victims of the Holocaust because they lacked the essential element of choice in their deaths. Since they did not die because of their beliefs but because of the accident of their birth as Jews (or as children or grandchildren of Jews), a new category of martyrdom, a new language, had to be invented.

Toward a Solution

There is no conflict between describing the uniqueness of the Jewish experience during the Holocaust and the *inclusion* of other victims of Nazism. In fact, the examination of all victims is not only politically desirable but pedagogically mandatory if we are to demonstrate the claim of uniqueness. History should guide the portrayal of all victims of Nazism – Jews and non-Jews. There are three historical dimensions to the question of uniqueness.

Firstly, the goal of the Holocaust was unprecedented. Never before did a state sponsor a systematic, bureaucratic extermination of an entire people in a quasi-apocalyptic act promising national salvation. Nazi Germany prioritized the murder of Jews over the war effort.

Methodologically, the Holocaust was without parallel. Raul Hilberg traces the process of extermination from definition to expropriation to concentration to deportation to extermination. Each step was part of a disciplined program borrowing on past policies but breaking new ground, shattering previous boundaries – moral, political, psychological, and religious – and overcoming the inertia of an entrenched bureaucracy, civilian as well as military. The end result was the creation of new instruments of destruction; the Nazis created *l'universe concentrainaire,* which Hannah Arendt called a "society of total domination," where Fackenheim's *musselman* (the walking dead) inhabit Wiesel's "kingdom of night." Langer speaks of the "death of choice," and Primo Levi writes about a "new language of atrocity."

Finally, the results of the Holocaust were 6 million dead, 1 million of them children – an entire world destroyed, a culture uprooted, and mankind left with new thresholds of inhumanity.

In order to demonstrate each dimension of the uniqueness, the plight of all the Nazi victims must be understood. How does one explain the systematic genocide of an entire people without contrasting the Jewish experience with the horrendous plight of the Polish people?

Unlike the Jews, Poles were consigned by the Nazis to subservience, not destruction. The Polish intelligentsia was annihilated so that Polish culture could be dominated. Gifted Polish children were aryanized, kidnapped, and brought to Germany for adoption by "pure Aryan" families. Thus, the Polish future was mortgaged.

Unlike the Poles, all Jews were condemned to death and not just a political, social, or intellectual elite. From Albert Einstein to Mottle the tailor, the Jew was considered the enemy. All Jewish blood was to be eliminated. Thus, even blond, blue-eyed, brilliant Jewish children were sent off to be destroyed.

Gypsies shared many but not all of the horrors imposed on Jews. Romani were killed in some countries but not in others. The fate of the rural Romani often differed from that of their urban counterparts. By contrast, the murder of Jews was a priority in every country; the Nazis pressed the bureaucracy to process Jews for the "Final Solution." Even though the Romani were subject to gassing and other forms of extermination, the number of Gypsies was not as vast, and individual death by gassing was far less certain than it was for Jews. This is not to diminish or minimize Gypsy suffering, which was intense, sustained, and harsh, but to focus on those dimensions of the Holocaust that were unique.

Like the Romani, homosexuals were arrested and incarcerated; similarly, many Ukrainians were sent to concentration camps, where they were jailed as prisoners of war, yet a Ukrainian or a homosexual could hope to outlive the Nazis merely by surviving. In contrast, all Jews lived under an imminent sentence of death. The ovens and gas chambers were primarily restricted to Jews. An apparatus originally designed for the mentally retarded and the emotionally disturbed consumed the Jews, although in all likelihood this destruction would not have ceased when the last Jew was killed had the Nazis won both the World War and the War Against the Jews.

Contra Bauer, the inclusion of non-Jews is neither a convenience nor a bow to the realities of pluralistic American life but an intellectual, historical, and pedagogical prerequisite to conveying the truth of what occurred in the Holocaust. Historical accuracy should unite ethnic communities (who wish their dead to be remembered) with Jewish survivors (who appropriately want the Judeo-centric nature of the experience to be told). Particularity need not be sacrificed to false universalism.

Bohdan Wytwytzky, a young philosopher of Ukrainian ancestry from Columbia University, has offered a compelling image for describing the Holocaust. He refers to the many circles of hell in Dante's *Inferno*. The Jews occupied the center of hell, with the concentric rings extending outward to incorporate many other victims much as waves spread outward with diminishing intensity from a stone tossed into a lake. In order to comprehend the Jewish center, we must fully probe the ripple effects as well as the indisputable core.

In arming themselves to protect the uniqueness of the Holocaust, many defenders of the faith (rather than the fact) have shied away from comparisons with other instances of subjugation or mass murder. Such comparisons do not innately obscure the uniqueness of the Holocaust; they clarify it. For example, inclusion of the Armenian experience in discussing the Holocaust does not detract from the Holocaust's uniqueness but deepens our moral sensitivity while sharpening our perception. Additionally, such inclusions display generosity of spirit and ethical integrity. We should let our sufferings, however incommensurate, unite us in condemnation of inhumanity rather than divide us in a calculus of calamity.

The analogies between the Armenian genocide and the Holocaust teach a number of moral lessons. For example, Hitler used the world's indifference to Armenian suffering to silence opposition to his plans for the Poles. The Armenian genocide assured Hitler that negative consequences would not greet his actions. Likewise, the memory of the Armenian genocide prompted Henry Morgenthau, Jr., to confront President Roosevelt with evidence of American inaction during the Holocaust. Henry Morgenthau, Sr., had been the American ambassador to Turkey during the Armenian massacres, and his namesake, the secretary of the treasury, remembered his father's example and acted responsibly. In the same manner, the Jewish resistance fighters at Bialystok invoked the memory of Musa Dag, the Armenian uprising, in fighting for freedom and honor. The Holocaust can become a symbolic orienting event in human history that can prevent recurrence.

Common to all these examples are two principles for dealing with events analogous but not equivalent to the Holocaust. The analogies must be historically authentic, and they must illuminate other dimensions of the Holocaust and the analogous event. If these principles are followed, we need not fear engaging in analogies that illumine scholarship and memory. Comparison will neither trivialize nor dejudaize the Holocaust.

3. Public Commemoration of the Holocaust

Scores of works present liturgies of Holocaust commemoration, but few have examined the ceremonies critically. This chapter is the first analysis of state-sponsored Holocaust commemorations initiated in America. Among the problems considered here is the ambivalence felt by survivors of the Holocaust, along with the rest of American Jewry, who seek a national imprimatur for their day of mourning yet fear dilution and dejudaization once commemoration leaves the confines of communal observance.

For two hundred years, the modern Jew faced two choices: self-imposed ghettoization, or the strict separation of Jewish life from the public domain. Our generation has the opportunity to reverse the rules of postemancipation Jewish life; Jewish communal engagement in politics and public life (manifested in events such as civic commemorations of the Holocaust) should be welcomed.

There are three separate but intersecting histories of the Holocaust that bear commemoration: those of the perpetrators, the bystanders, and the victims. American Jews can claim two of these histories as heirs of the victims and fellow countrymen (or descendants) of the bystanders. Israeli Jews relate most basically to the history of the victims, yet they have felt uncomfortable with some aspects of that identification because of a national posture of military strength. Israelis also participate in the bystanders' legacy because the Yishuv (the prestate Jewish community in Palestine) was relatively inactive during the late 1930s and early 1940s.

Christianity must accept two histories. Self-proclaimed Christians not only were bystanders but were among the perpetrators, and the choice of Jews as victims stemmed either directly or indirectly from the church's treatment of Judaism in its liturgy and theology. Authentic Christian commemoration of the Holocaust must confront the role of the perpetrator as well as that of the bystander before it takes refuge in those few precious incidents where Christians bore witness to their faith in solidarity with Jews. These moments, however luminous or instructive, should not obscure the more serious issue of Christian perpetration (rather than victimization) during the Holocaust.

Governments, too, have an agenda for commemoration. The Holocaust was committed as an act of state – not as an outlaw phenomenon but as a thoroughly disciplined, bureaucratic process that used all of the powers and instrumentalities available to modern governments. Nonperpetrator governments were bystanders that tacitly sanctioned Hitler's program by silence or inaction if not by participation in the Nazi destruction of Jews.

The themes and modes of commemoration chosen by each of the parties is dictated by the specific behavior that it wishes to confront or avoid. The agenda is set not only by hopes for the future but by past experience. The struggle to recall the Holocaust is never simple. Cognitively dissonant experience – suffering so great that it threatens to devour human meaning – challenges normative concepts and so undermines the corpus of shared values held sacred by the institutions that seek to commemorate the Holocaust.

Before 1979, the commemorative task was limited to the Jewish community, which had developed distinctive patterns of Holocaust observance, and to those churches and Christian organizations that shared a sensitivity to Jewish experience. Aside from the National Day of Remembrance in Israel (Yom Hashoah), civic remembrances were virtually nonexistent and interfaith Holocaust remembrance services were rare.

For centuries Jewish tradition had reserved national days of mourning for other tragic events, such as Tisha B'Av, which commemorates the destruction of the first and second Temples in Jerusalem. Unlike the religious character of Tisha B'Av, a manifestly secular tone developed for Yom Hashoah. In Israel a communitywide commemoration of the Holocaust is sponsored by the municipality or the state, and in America local Jewish federations or community relations councils foster programs that include memorial prayers, candle lighting, songs of the Partisans and concentration camps, and addresses citing a familiar litany of horrors as well as the lessons that undergird current commitments.

A few churches attempted to commemorate the Holocaust within the ordinary religious context of Sunday morning worship. By contrast, Jewish Holocaust commemorations usually did not take place within regular prayer services, even if a prayer or two was added to sabbath services preceding Yom Hashoah or to the Yom Kippur Martyrology (as has been done in recent prayer books of both the Conservative and Reform movements).[1] Artistic and cinematographic treatments of the Holocaust were generally not incorporated into such observances even though religious prohibitions (such as Sabbath restrictions) would not have precluded alternate media. By and large, observance of Yom Hashoah remains monovalent, in one-dimensional media.[2]

The appointment of the President's Commission on the Holocaust in 1979 presented new possibilities for the commemoration of the Holocaust. The Commission's central charge, "to recommend an appropriate national memorial to the victims of the Holocaust," ostensibly had little to do with commemorative services. Senator John Danforth, an ordained Episcopal minister, was so moved by his encounter with the Holocaust, provided in part by the April 1978 television airing of *Holocaust,* that he proposed National Days of Remembrance for Victims of the Holocaust on April 28–29, 1979 (the thirty-fourth anniversary of the liberation of Dachau by American troops). At the time of this proposal, Danforth was unaware of the existence of Yom Hashoah (on the twenty-seventh of the Hebrew month Nisan), or of White House plans for the establishment of a presidential commission. Danforth's suggestion for National Days of Remembrance was later incorporated into President Carter's charge in Executive Order 12903. The final decision to hold a week-long commemoration allowed the program to coincide with Yom Hashoah while also accommodating Sunday church participation. The commemorative week became a cornerstone of the Holocaust Commission's recommendation, its *Report to the President,* and the subsequent plans of its successor body, the United States Holocaust Memorial Council.

The mandate of the Commission provided new possibilities for the scope of commemorative activities. It opened up the whole realm of secular society for Holocaust commemoration. In its initial year, the Commission established a national civil commemoration of the Holocaust; statewide observances modeled after the central national event; proclamations of Days of Remembrance by every level of national, state, and local government; school and library displays of Holocaust-related material; media recognition of the Days of Remembrance through television programming, public service announcements, editorials and op-ed pieces, talk shows and other radio broadcasts. Secular attention also generated a significant increase in the number of churches and synagogues commemorating the Holocaust. Despite limited staff and resources, the Commission was able to provide viable models for following years.

Elie Wiesel, chairman of the President's Commission on the Holocaust and the United States Holocaust Memorial Council, suggested the conceptual model for the national commemoration. He felt that a joint session of Congress, addressed by the president of the United States and a survivor, might prove an appropriate forum. Yet, between the novelist's imagination and the realities of American public life, there remained a considerable gap. James Blanchard, then a promising young congressman (and now governor of Michigan), bridged that gap. Blanchard recalled to the Commission's staff his most moving experience in Washington, the bicentennial visit of the Magna Carta from England to the United States. This sacred text of democracy was transferred by the queen of England to the American people for the bicentennial year in a meeting of both the House and the Senate and the president of the United States in the Capitol Rotunda. The Commission staff, under my direction, developed a similar program for Days of Remembrance. Its key ingredients included a noon meeting in the Capitol Rotunda; addresses by the president, the vice-president, and the chairman of the President's Commission; memorial prayers and the kaddish; songs of the Partisans and *Ani Maamin;* candle lighting and a benediction. The ceremony lasted less than forty-five minutes. It was designed for simplicity, emotional impact, and beauty. The implementation of the ceremony

required a joint resolution of Congress and White House cooperation. Scheduled for Yom Hashoah (which fell on April 24, 1979),
the ceremony sparked statewide commemorations in Connecticut, New Jersey, and Minnesota. (These states were the residences
of particularly active members of the Commission who, in cooperation with the national staff, undertook major initiatives.) After
ten years, each of the fifty states now holds civic commemorations – often in state legislative chambers. Hundreds of cities and
towns throughout the country sponsor local civic commemorations. In 1989, more than a million people attended Holocaust
commemorations.

Two complications developed in planning the national ceremony, both of which were to have implications for the work of
the Commission not only in its commemorative activities but in
the planning of the actual memorial. By coincidence, April 24 was
the annual memorial day for victims of the Armenian genocide
during World War I. No event in history is so closely analogous
to the Holocaust, though certainly not equivalent. Each year April
24 is marked by special prayers in memory of the Armenian dead
and by a ceremony on Capitol Hill used as countertestimony to
the Turkish denial of the crime. The Commission faced the choice
of including the Armenians within the Holocaust ceremony and
thus running the risk of "universalizing" the Holocaust, or of having the Armenians stand outside, opposite the ceremony, while
Jewish dead were recalled.

In addition, the Commission had to grapple with the divisive
issue of how to commemorate the Nazi murder of other people –
Poles, Gypsies, Ukrainians, and various European ethnics – who
perceived themselves as victims of the Holocaust. Wiesel and the
survivors feared that the inclusion of non-Jews in the Days of Remembrance would dejudaize the Holocaust. Furthermore, anger
at the collaboration between Eastern European ethnics and the
Nazis in the "Final Solution" was intensely felt by Jewish survivors. In 1979, the Commission decided to invite Armenian participation as a link to other acts of massive annihilation but to stress
the targeting of Jews for total annihilation. In subsequent years,
without fanfare or controversy, representatives of Eastern European ethnic communities have been invited to participate and indi-

vidual non-Jews have been honored for heroic acts in preserving Jewish lives.

Just before the 1979 ceremony, the Turkish government contacted the White House, objecting to any reference to the Armenian genocide. The Turks threatened that delicate negotiations between the Carter administration and the Turkish government might be adversely affected or that Israeli–Turkish relations could be harmed. A peculiar kinship between the Armenian and the Jewish experience was sensed by some people. If the German government had followed the Turkish example and tried to deny the crime of its predecessors, the American government might have been similarly reluctant to confront the reality of the Holocaust for fear of offending our German allies in NATO. A compromise was reached by the White House staff in which the president would only make reference to the Armenian experience in an elliptical fashion. The ceremony proceeded without complication, though not without considerable controversy in its aftermath, as the judgments that had been made were evaluated and their full implications understood.

Elie Wiesel addressed the Capitol Rotunda ceremony as the chairman of the President's Commission on the Holocaust. Wiesel's insight and eloquence as a speaker were enhanced by his presidential appointment. The distinction between the charisma of office and the charisma of person, like the tension between the Jewish memorial and an American national memorial, would remain unresolved throughout Wiesel's eight-year tenure as chairman. Seven years later, Wiesel tested the limits of his two roles when he used the Rotunda ceremony to plead against President Ronald Reagan's impending trip to Bitburg. In what many have called Wiesel's finest hour, he brilliantly walked the tightrope, morally challenging the president without offending him personally, talking in the language of history and memory against temporary political accommodations.

There are several perils to a national civic commemoration, which are now apparent after a decade of experience. First of all, there is the question of control. When, in his address at the Capitol Rotunda, President Carter referred to the Holocaust as "the systematic and state-sponsored extermination of six million Jews and

five million others by the Nazis and their collaborators during
World War II," this definition of the Holocaust made many survivors on the Commission uncomfortable for it included non-Jews
among the victims of the Holocaust. As we have seen, Yehuda
Bauer cast aspersions at the Commission's entire enterprise on the
basis of the president's words. Subsequently, President Ronald
Reagan, in his initial Holocaust commemoration speech, quoted
Pope Pius XII as an authority on the implications of the Holocaust, offending all who knew of the pope's inaction and acquies-
cence, if not collaboration, with Nazi persecution. Although
Reagan brought the full weight of his personal experience and
prestige of office to bear against those who would deny that the
Holocaust ever occurred, he also asserted, contrary to all historical
evidence, that the German people had been unaware of what was
happening in the concentration camps. Reagan said:

> I remember seeing the first film that came in when the war
> was still on, when our troops had come upon the first camps
> and had entered those camps. . . . in one of those camps,
> there was a nearby town, and the people were ordered to
> come and look at what had been going on, and to see them.
> And the reaction of horror on their faces was the greatest
> proof that they had not been conscious of what was happen-
> ing so near to them.

The rewriting of history implicit in the Bitburg controversy began
a full four years earlier in Reagan's assertion of German ignorance.

Reagan's personal recollections have also been challenged. According to a series of newspaper accounts, during a conversation
with Simon Wiesenthal and Rabbi Marvin Hier in the Oval Office, Reagan indicated he had actually been to the camps, a claim
that the record of his World War II service does not substantiate.
At another time, Reagan is reported to have claimed that he edited
raw footage from the camps, an assertion that Lou Cannon, a
Washington Post reporter and Reagan's longtime political biogra-
pher, considers dubious.

The president's words, a governor's speech, or a mayor's address are written by speechwriters who are not necessarily knowl-
edgeable or sensitive concerning the Holocaust. "Talking points"

are sometimes solicited from informed parties, but ultimate control lies in the hands of the speaker and not those who would seek his sanction for their sentiments. General attention and media coverage naturally focus on the words of powerful officeholders and not on survivors giving authentic testimony.

The Holocaust cannot be thrust into the political arena without Jews losing a measure of control over the way in which it is handled. On the other hand, the scope of a national occasion with an address on the Holocaust provides an opportunity to sensitize officials and their staffs, as well as the general public, to the Holocaust and its implications for national policy. Furthermore, it fosters the possibility that influential people will be moved by the event and thus support important action on behalf of Jews and others. For example, as a result of his participation in the 1979 Holocaust commemoration, former vice-president Walter Mondale began his speech at the Geneva Conference on the Cambodian and Vietnamese boat people by evoking memories of the failure of Evian in 1938. "The memory of inaction then should spur responsible action now," Mondale said. Similarly, President Reagan announced at the 1981 Holocaust commemoration that he would press for human rights at every international forum. (Reagan's heartfelt statement surprised the White House press office, which later felt obliged to qualify the remark because it was perceived as a departure from the administration's policy. Still, in pursuit of consistency, actions are frequently changed to fit words as well as vice versa.)

Politics has its own dynamic; in entering the political realm, ethnic groups run the risk of losses as well as gains. The Holocaust either can be preserved as the sacred domain of a particular community without dilution and distortion, or can become part of a wider consciousness. If Jews choose to avoid all risks, they cannot bemoan the world's ignorance or indifference. In deciding to enlarge the circle of discourse, we can take heart in realizing that the event itself may provide significant limitations.

The other major risk in public commemoration is that the Holocaust will be Americanized – that is, reshaped to participate in the fundamental tale of pluralism, tolerance, democracy, and human rights that America tells about itself. These universal values can be reaffirmed not only by recalling the Holocaust but by remembering other instances of injustice and indignity. They are the values that all Americans share. The Jewish experience of suffering – the particular, incomparable tragedy that befell the Jewish people alone during World War II – might be tamed if it is used only as an instrument to reinforce traditional American principles.

National commemoration of the Holocaust always entails the possibility of politicalization, in both the United States and Israel. Former Israeli prime minister Menachem Begin invoked the Holocaust to gain sympathy for his hardline position toward territorial concessions. Jimmy Carter may have used the formation of the Commission on the Holocaust to pacify Begin and the American Jewish community, who were opposed to his decision to sell F-15s to Saudi Arabia. Three years later in 1981, Reagan's participation in the national ceremony may also have been designed to offset his sale of AWACS and F-15 add-ons to Saudi Arabia. In the East Room of the White House, Elie Wiesel told Reagan and the country: "We all know that your being here, Mr. President, is not a ceremonial gesture but an expression of your sense of history and your dream of a future with hope and dignity for the American nation and for all mankind." Despite this eloquence, sober political motives may affect the nature and timing of presidential participation.

Jewish tradition has always recognized mixed motives and sought to utilize them in positive ways; the rabbis have continually negotiated between realpolitik and prophetic demands. They taught: "That which is originally done not for its own sake may come to be done for its own sake."

Civic commemorations raise the issues associated with the Holocaust for a constituency that would not have been reached through parochial commemoration. For example, during the week of Yom Hashoah a young Roman Catholic legislator in Boston spoke of how moved he was by the story of a survivor who taught him "the purpose for which laws are enacted, the reason for his choice of a political career." In the state senate of Connecticut, the governor responded in tears to another survivor. In Washington, a Holocaust commemoration was able to unite feuding black and Jewish lawmakers, establishing a sense of depth and integrity previously absent from their conversations.

In sum, public commemorations of the Holocaust maximize cultural impact while increasing the danger of distortion or misuse. Secularization and a certain loss of control are inevitable. Purists rightfully advise caution, insisting that the political price must be reevaluated at every juncture. On the other hand, silence invites historical ignorance and the perils of repetition.

During the second half of the twentieth century the Jewish people reentered history by assuming land and power, a state and an army. They turned their attention away from what Franz Rosenzweig called "the gaze of eternity" and – in a commitment born of anguish and hope – embraced the vicissitudes of history. In the process, our people have been transformed, our traditions tested, our values both strengthened and threatened. The Holocaust Council also represents – on a significantly smaller scale – the same movement into history, the interaction with power and politics, the struggle to maintain integrity in a world of contradictions. The timid advise us not to tamper with the sacred mystery of the Holocaust. The Holocaust has moved beyond the ghetto and entered the mainstream; our task now is not evasion but responsible address.

4. Is the Centrality of the Holocaust Overemphasized? Two Dialogues

Dialogue has long been an indispensable form of theological engagement. This chapter presents two dialogues. In the first, Arnold Wolf (then at Yale University) and I debate the appropriate place of the Holocaust in American Jewish life. In the second dialogue, I respond to David Weiss, an Orthodox rabbi, who argues that the Holocaust should have no impact on Jewish faith.

Both Wolf and Weiss seek to minimize the implications of the Holocaust by removing it from the public life and religious faith of contemporary Jews. Weiss's defense of the covenant's eternity is the antithesis of my own views that the relationship between God and the people of Israel evolves in time and is transformed by history, most especially by the revolutionary events of recent Jewish experience.

"The Centrality of the Holocaust is a Mistake," by Arnold Jacob Wolf

There is one thing that is worse than too much talk about the Holocaust and that is hearing people say there is too much talk. That is my situation.

When I left Congregation Solel in Chicago, I expected to be offered hundreds of jobs, but I was offered two. One was with the commission directly related to the Holocaust – because I had spent fifteen years producing a congregational study of the Holocaust, which was unusual, perhaps unique, in the country, and I involved Elie Wiesel and Raul Hilberg in that study as long as twenty-two years ago. The other job I was offered was at B'nai

Arnold Jacob Wolf is Rabbi of KAM Isaiah Israel Congregation. This dialogue was held at the annual meeting of the B'nai B'rith Hillel Foundation Board in 1980. At that time, Rabbi Wolf was the Hillel Director at Yale University.

B'rith Hillel at Yale. In a way, the choice I faced is symbolic of what I have to say: The problem is an overweening concern with the Holocaust as opposed to other concerns.

The city of New Haven is munificent in its support of Holocaust activities. There is now money for Holocaust studies when, for example, at Yale Hillel we could not cover the last check of our student assistant who gets $4,000 a year, and we could not keep an administrative secretary who had been with us ten years without a raise.

There is a competition, and this is a time of limited funds, limited personnel, and limited decisions. You cannot do everything, and it is a simple fact that in New Haven, the Jewish community of 22,000 spends about ten times as much money on the Holocaust memorial as it does on all the college students in New Haven. I think that is shocking. I think that is what Professor Emil Fackenheim called a posthumous victory for Hitler.

Yale University is finally creating a Jewish major – perhaps because Harvard did it earlier. So Yale is out to raise money and has been offered $1 million – allegedly in cash – if the first endowed chair of Jewish studies will be in Holocaust studies.

Is it right that one endowed chair in all of Jewish literature, philosophy, religion, and thought should be for Holocaust studies? That whichever way they decide, they're wrong? That's an impossible dilemma. Either they produce an emphasis which is bizarre, and I think absolutely unjustifiable, or they refuse to teach a perfectly legitimate subject which is the only one at this stage that they can get fully funded.

The community is saying: "We have money for Holocaust, and that's all." We have decreasing funds for almost everything else you can think of and certainly for Jewish studies in Midrash or Talmud or philosophy or even Bible, but we have $1 million if you're willing to teach the Holocaust.

And incidentally, we *are* teaching the Holocaust; we have had seminars on the Holocaust every term. We could not have a seminar on a kibbutz, which I was trying to arrange for eight years. We could not have seminar in a biography of Moses Maimonides, Rabbi Akiva, or Theodore Herzl. But there is a clientele for Holocaust studies, which excludes other alternatives and which is producing, counterproductively, a sense that this is what we are in the business of doing.

My colleague from the Anti-Defamation League spends most of his time talking to me about the Holocaust. A few years ago he had a different agenda. I cannot believe that the Holocaust is the most important subject for the work of anti-defamation in Connecticut.

It seems to me the Holocaust is being sold – it is not being taught.

Another problem stemming from the centrality of the Holocaust is that we compare Yasir Arafat to Hitler and Eichmann. That is a dangerous perception. Whatever is wrong with the Palestine Liberation Organization – God knows there is plenty wrong with it – the model of the 6 million is the wrong model. That model does not refer to a conflict over land, over place, over owning the same thing. The PLO's war is not genocidal in the same way. It is a war like the one in Algeria, something like other territorial conflicts, only more bitter – and for us, terribly dangerous. But the model is not the model of conflict over territory, it is the model of extermination camps and gas chambers.

Arafat may be more dangerous than Hitler and he may succeed where Hitler failed, not because he is Hitler but precisely because he is not. Because the world understands that something very different is going on. And if we say we are entitled to the land of Israel because of the Holocaust, we deny a hundred years of Zionism, we repudiate the second aliyah (the immigration to Israel that began in 1903 after the Kishinev pogrom), and the Arabs can correctly say to us, "Look, if Hitler did you in, have your Jewish state in Bavaria."

Our claim to the land of Israel has nothing to do with the Holocaust. As Martin Buber said, the great tragedy is that because of the Holocaust, we entered our own land through the wrong doorway.

But everything gets assimilated to Holocaust: the problem in Israel, problems in the United States. I have heard Leonid Brezhnev and Stokely Carmichael and every two-bit antisemite called if not Hitler, then Eichmann. The world begins to stop listening.

If everything is Holocaust, nothing is Holocaust.

If everything is assimilated to the one great event in Jewish history, then there are no other great events in Jewish history. And if the New Haven Jewish community, for example, has all of its communal meetings at a memorial for the 6 million, what does a seven-year-old think Jewish history is all about? He thinks it is all about Auschwitz, but it isn't; because the Holocaust is only one dreadfully important, crucial, but limited part of a three-millennia history.

We have no memorials to the pioneers of Israel or to the rabbis of the Talmud, or even to the patriarchs and matriarchs. The only memorial in New Haven, and in most other places, if there is a memorial at all, is to the 6 million. We have nothing else we want to say to the world so clearly, so powerfully, so artistically, and so expensively.

I could talk about what this has done to Jewish theology: the dreadful and ludicrous chapter of the "Death of God" theology was an extrapolation from the Holocaust. I could talk about what it does to individuals. When I write the head of an organization a long, serious letter about what I think the problems of Hillel are, no answers come. But when he hears that I gave a sermon somewhere in an obscure Reform temple that gets reported in garbled fashion, that sermon, because it's about the Holocaust, produces a long, complicated letter and hearings and God knows what else. Because the Holocaust is where it's at. Because the Holocaust sets off nerve endings. Because we somehow think it is more important even than the work we do, the life-or-death work we do for hundreds and hundreds of Jewish students. If Cynthia Ozick is right that the whole world wants the Jews dead, they will get it. If everybody is Hitler, we are finished. If we have no allies and only enemies, we cannot survive. No matter what we do, no matter how big our Zionism or how great our fund-raising or how extreme our celebration of the Holocaust might be.

Zionism is about finding alliances, as Herzl knew from the very beginning. It is about working with other kinds of people and as David Ben-Gurion knew, even German people. It is not grinding in the face of the gentile world its crime against the Jews. Of course we are not to forget, and we will not forget, and I promise

I will not forget, but if I have one thing to say to a Christian, it will not be about the Holocaust. Maybe that will be the second thing or the third. But the first thing will be about the Bible, it will be about the common problematic, and it will be about the people whom both of us work together to help.

There is something in the Christian world that likes this emphasis on the Holocaust, that likes seeing the Jews as perpetual victim, or alternatively, as in Israel against the Palestinians, as the opposite of a victim: a terrorizer. And we must find a way of saying we are not merely victims, and we are not merely persecutors; we are people with a tradition of which we are proud – a creative tradition in which we were not passive but active, in which we taught the world some of its greatest lessons. That is what we have to say to the world. And not only, and not especially, what the world did to us.

The greatest survivors hardly ever talked about the Holocaust. Martin Buber, Abraham Heschel, and S. Y. Agnon only obliquely, sensitively, carefully wrote about the world in which the Holocaust took place. They did not enter into the great liturgy, into the great proliferation of literature about the Holocaust itself. Perhaps because they thought it could not yet be done, perhaps because they thought it could not be done in the way others have tried to do it, perhaps because they felt the best answer to the Holocaust is Hasidism and Bible and Talmud and the literature of Eastern Europe before Hitler and *Eretz Yisrael*. And if they thought that, I do too. I believe we have a great deal beyond the Holocaust, a great agenda, and it's time we got to it.

In Response: The Lessons of the Holocaust Are All-Important

If there is one thing worse than talking too much about the Holocaust, it is talking too little, and the one thing worse than talking too little is talking incorrectly.

Why does the Holocaust have such a grip on the consciousness and imagination of the Jewish people, particularly since 1967? Perhaps we should ask the question the other way: what incredible repression would it take to diminish the importance of an event that resulted in the destruction of one-third of one's people? When I speak to Christians, as well as Jews, the Holocaust is among the most important items I raise.

It seems that the grass is always greener on the other side of the fence. I spent the last couple of weeks trying to raise $4,000 for the publication of the best single curriculum available on the Holocaust – the best in English, Hebrew, French, or German. From Arnold Wolf's perspective, there's too much money in Holocaust studies; from my perspective, there's not enough. The money that's available is not being used correctly.

It is a misstatement to say that the Jewish community has spent too much money on the Holocaust – ten times as much on the memorial in New Haven, Connecticut, for example, as on Jewish studies there. The memorial was a one-time project, a one-time event, and Jewish studies is an ongoing commitment. The educational budgets year in and year out will exceed the expenditure for the memorial when capitalized over a few years. I see neither an abundance of funding for Holocaust studies, nor do I see that the Holocaust is somehow edging out and destroying all sorts of other Jewish activities.

I taught Judaica in a religion department and offered twenty-three courses over a five-year period. Of these, only three were on different aspects of the Holocaust. At Wesleyan University, and at other universities with which I am familiar, the Holocaust is taught within the context of many other Judaic offerings to stress continuities as well as discontinuities. For example, one of the opening lectures in a course I give on the Holocaust deals with the relationship of the Holocaust to all previous forms of antisemitism. I don't view the Holocaust within the tradition of previous manifestations of antisemitism but as a distinctly modern, unprecedented outbreak. The Holocaust took place within the law, using all the instrumentalities of the modern state and advanced technology. Furthermore, it was the one time in which Jews were killed because they were born Jews, born of Jewish ancestors, rather than because of the identity they had or the views and religious affirmations they held. Throughout the rest of Jewish history, Jews had alternatives: they could leave, they could convert, or they could choose martyrdom. The Holocaust does not involve martyrdom in its classical sense because for most victims there was no choice. The most poignant example of this lack of choice is the story retold by Marcus Bloch of a French boy, seven years of age, on his way to Auschwitz, who turned to his father and said, "What is a Jew?" His father responded, "All my life I tried to protect you from that reality."

Though the Holocaust is unprecedented in Jewish history, our tradition provides avenues for approaching the tragedy. I backed into study of the Holocaust after studying Jeremiah and Yochanan Ben Zakkai. For years, I taught Yochanan Ben Zakkai, the rabbi who made a revolutionary change in Jewish life in response to the destruction of the second Temple. I still read Jeremiah, and he remains my favorite prophet because he was the man who saw catastrophe, tried to prevent it, and compassionately responded to it when it did take place.

I agree with Arnold Wolf's point with respect to the erosion of the power of language. If everything is a holocaust, then nothing is *the* Holocaust, and if we flatten the meaning of the word through abuse, we ultimately destroy the significance of the code word "Holocaust."

For example, the PLO should not be seen from the perspective of the Holocaust, for thankfully it lacks the power to enact its genocidal proclamations. Were it to abandon the most vulgar aspects of its charter – that the creation of the State of Israel be rendered null and void and that the Jewish state be entirely obliterated – the Jewish community might be able to assess its grievances and its aspirations.* The threat made in 1967 by Ahmed Shukeiry, that the Arabs would throw the Jews into the sea, to my mind echoed a subliminal message: one generation by fire, the next gen-

---

Although Yasir Arafat recognized Israel in December 1988, and indicated a willingness to negotiate with it, the PLO charter has (to date) not been changed.

eration by water. Were the PLO to move away from speaking of genocide, one could deal with it on a different level, and that would be healthier for Jews and Palestinians.

One reason that memorials are built to the Holocaust is because we feel compelled to produce something concrete to commemorate a world that disappeared. Jews should aim for a living memorial, not just a physical memorial – a legacy of teaching, learning, and scholarship, a memorial that responds to the needs of the living, that takes the memory of those who died and uses it to inform our lives. Memorials are being built as an inadequate response to an overpowering sense of loss.

We all understand that Jewish life is vulnerable. We all understand that we live in a peculiar time. We had once imagined that the Zionist revolution of statehood, of sovereignty and power, would end Jewish vulnerability. But it has not. Israel has altered the conditions under which we confront our vulnerability and the way in which we respond to that vulnerability. Although vulnerability remains the fundamental condition of Jewish life, victimhood does not.

We are wrong when we legitimate ourselves as victims par excellence by using the Holocaust as the example, as if victimhood conferred some blessing, some virtue. Everything I understand about Jewish tradition says to me that suffering demands a response, an attempt to alleviate suffering.

My professional and personal encounter with the Holocaust does not blind me to the vast, rich inheritance of Jewish religious, poetic, philosophical, and theological literature; nor do I think that the many people who have done serious Jewish scholarship in the Holocaust have ended up excluding the rest of tradition. We may now have a paucity of authentic spiritual teachers in the Jewish community, and the Bible is frequently presented in a way that lacks both depth and excitement, yet this is not because able thinkers are distracted by the Holocaust. There are gifted teachers who have struggled to understand the Holocaust, who have come to terms with it as they confronted the rest of Jewish tradition for language, and they've gone to it for bewilderment.

It is not true that such masters as Martin Buber, Abraham Heschel, and S. Y. Agnon did not deal with the Holocaust. Buber's first response to the Holocaust was in a significant work called *The Eclipse of God,* which is theologically still one of the most substantive works dealing with the Holocaust. Buber died in 1965 at the age of eighty-seven, so one can permit him the liberty of a less monumental undertaking, given the limits of both his age and endurance as well as the agenda he had set for himself. Abraham Joshua Heschel also responded to the Holocaust. In 1951, he published *The Earth Is the Lord's,* a eulogy for Eastern European Jewry. In his last years, Heschel again returned to the Holocaust, although unfortunately that writing was his most unsuccessful. He borrowed some of the images suggested by Elie Wiesel, but he was basically unable to fit the Holocaust into his various models of the religious life. Heschel's difficulties in addressing the Holocaust as a whole correlated with his problems in dealing with death. Even his famous essay on death is inadequate, lacking his usual depth. The best treatment of the Holocaust by S. Y. Agnon appears in a short but effective story in which he imaginatively returns to his village on the night he hears that the town was decimated; he ends the tale in madness.

If the Holocaust is going to take the place of the rest of Jewish history, then we have given Hitler not only a posthumous victory but the power to determine our future and to define the limits of our concerns. I don't think that this has happened empirically or philosophically – or that it should happen. Nevertheless, the Holocaust, along with the rebirth of Israel, is one of the two central events of modern Jewish history, central events that involve the totality of Jewish history and that chart all subsequent directions. We only avoid struggling with the meaning and implications of these events at our peril. We can avoid overemphasizing the Holocaust by using it as part of a dialectic that speaks to the totality of Jewish history. Beyond our study of the Holocaust within Jewish history and theology, we must learn political lessons from the Holocaust about the innately frightening aspects of modernity and the contemporary capacity to inflict death and destruction.

I was involved with planning a trip to Cambodia for Senator John Danforth, an Episcopal minister who studied the Holocaust after viewing the TV Holocaust film. Because of this exposure to the Holocaust, Danforth said, "I cannot sit here without going to see what's happening there." The memory of what he knew about the Holocaust has energized him to become one of the national leaders trying to alleviate the suffering in Cambodia and Thailand.

I fear that the Holocaust may become a new threshold, a precedent, for what people can do to each other. That is the most important reason we must share the lessons of the Holocaust, integrating them into our collective being so that we become sensitive to danger signals and effective in prevention.

After the Holocaust, Another Covenant?
by David W. Weiss

The incumbency of a radically new Judaic theology has been argued with growing insistence during the past thirty years. Pivotal to the claim is the imputed uniqueness of the European holocaust[1] of 1939–45. The horror visited on the Jewish people during these years has been, it is claimed, a wholly singular experience, and one that signals the beginning of a new era. The classic Judaic delineation of the relationship between God and the House of Israel is no longer tenable, perhaps, indeed, has not been since the destruction of the second Temple and Jewish commonwealth. The covenant that was, or the illusion of this covenant, has been abrogated in the German death camps. What is demanded of the survivors is a new covenant, a unilateral, voluntary assertion by the

Professor David W. Weiss is the chairman of the Lautenberg Center for Tumor Immunology at the Hebrew University in Jerusalem. Born in Vienna, he came to the United States before the war. An Orthodox Jew and a distinguished scientist, Weiss writes often on religious issues. His essay represents the perspective of those religious Jews who seek to minimize the importance of the Holocaust as an event in Jewish history in order to diminish its religious significance.

This dialogue was first published in Sh'ma: A Journal of Jewish Responsibility, edited by Eugene Borowitz. For a more detailed exposition of Professor Weiss's views, the reader may consult his work The Wings of the Dove: Jewish Values, Science and Halachah (Washington, D.C.: B'nai B'rith Books, 1987). There are several minor errors in Weiss's essay, but the original is presented as published with permission of the author.

House of Israel of the will to continue Jewish existence in the face of an indifferent, changeable, or nonexistent deity.

I address myself not to the terrifying implications of the proposed new theology, nor make any attempt to analyze the diverse motivations of its proponents as I ask: Is the contention valid?

It is not, and I am at loss to comprehend the reasoning of serious thinkers who posit the view. Perhaps I do not have the privilege of saying this. I have not experienced in my body the suffering of European Jewry – although I lived nearly a year in Austria after the Anschluss until escaping, and lost all but my immediate family in the period that followed – and I may therefore lack a certain right, or authority, to speak. But then, perhaps the obligation to speak has not devolved on those not so seared, who still have speech.

The Holocaust of 1939–45 Was Not Unique

It may be that what transpired was unprecedented in scope, setting, and expectation. One would not have thought it possible that this could take place in mid-twentieth century, at the hands of a cultured nation, and to the apathy of the rest of the civilized world. But the uniqueness of these aspects of the Holocaust is debatable. A more sober estimation of the behavior of technologically advanced peoples before, during, and after the destruction of European Jewry, and in other regards, leaves less room for astonishment. Man has always given evidence of the potential for humanity and compassion, but the dominant theme of his record to the present is not undeserving of the epitomization *lupus est homo homini, no homo, quom qualis sit non novit.* The Jewish people have accepted, as part of their ancient covenant, the challenge of witness of greater possibilities.

For this we have suffered, horribly, uniquely, and repeatedly throughout postbiblical history. Whole regions have been devastated of their Jewish communities in recurrent, earlier holocausts; I employ that denotation advisedly. I doubt that the impact on individual Jew, or community, or a land of communities of devastation in the reaches all about was very different in the past than the impact now on world Jewry of ruin on a larger geographic and numerical scale. It is uncertain, too, whether the German attrition was in fact of a vastly different order proportionately than earlier desolation; there are data that suggest otherwise.

Theologically, religiously, it seems to be absurd to hold that the extirpation of Judea, Rhineland, or Southeastern European Jewry was a more acceptable experience than what transpired between 1939 and 1945. Is the vision of an infinite God who is Guardian of Israel less shaken by the annihilation of *only* a million Jews at the hands of the Romans, or *only* several hundred thousand each by crusaders, cossacks, haidamuks, than by the 6 million dead in German Europe? A god who plays these odds is not the God of Judaism. And Judaism has survived until 1939, as it shall now, without denying its God and the covenant with Him.

Individuals Choose; the People May Not

Certainly, this last havoc demands a searching, penetrating reaffirmation of faith and commitment, as there have been urgent gropings for renewed meaning in the wake of earlier holocausts. The striving for new perspectives and new apperceptions is indeed a constant demand of the spirit on every Jew, at all times. But a "new *covenant*," a "new *epoch*" – that is a closing of the book of Judaism. Whatever their sincerity, their love of Israel, their loyalties to Jewish practice, the prophets of the new covenant call not to a revitalization but to denial of the God of Israel and annulment of the Jew's raison d'être in the world. That, too, is not unique. Not all the gropings after preceding desolation remained anchored in the covenant that is. Those that were not, led into apostate movements and disappearance. The endeavor for new covenants today too shall fail, to be remembered as a tragic aberration. The *individual* Jew has choice before him. He can opt for the prototype antipodes of hasidism and of Sabbatean–Frankist oblivion, to add new dimensions and nuance to the mainstream of Judaism or to cut himself off.* The House of Israel has no such choice. Once initiated with the Patriarchs and reconfirmed by the assembled multitudes at Sinai, the

The Sabbatean movement was a heretical messianic sect of the seventeenth century that followed the "Mystical Messiah" Shabbetai Sevi. The Frankist movement comprised another heretical mystical movement, of the eighteenth century.

covenant is irrevocable. This is a principle of the faith of Judaism. It is put eloquently in *Midrash Rabbah* on Exodus 3:14:

> "I Shall Be As I Shall Be." Yohanan said: "I Shall Be As I Shall Be" to individuals, but for the community of Israel, I rule over them even if against their desire and will, even though they break their teeth, as it is said: "As I live, saith the Lord God, surely with a mighty hand and with an outstretched arm, and with fury poured out, will I be King over you." (Ezekiel 20: 33)

The commentary on the Midrash, *Matnat Kehunah*, amplifies: "The individual who desires and chooses Me, to him I shall be God; and if he does not so desire, it is given him to cast off the yoke; but to the community of Israel I do not give the option of casting off the yoke of heaven."

The advocates of new covenants will not halt the salvational history of the Jewish people, but they can add to the century's attritions. They must not go unchallenged, therefore. It must be told unequivocally: they are advocates not of a reaffirmed Judaism, but of something other than the religion eternal of a God eternal.

A Perspective of Holocausts

The Jew must struggle to come to grips with ravage and loss on two distinct levels, that of the People collectively and that of the individual.

For the People, the covenant is indissoluble, and its conditions have been spelled out:

> See, I have set before thee this day life and good, and death and evil . . . I command thee this day to love the Lord thy God, to walk in his ways, and to keep his commandments. . . . Then thou shalt live and the Lord thy God shall bless thee in the land into which thou goest. . . . But if thy heart turn away . . . and shalt worship other gods . . . I announce to you this day, that thou shalt surely perish, and that thou shalt not prolong your days upon the land. . . . I call heaven and earth to witness this day against you, that I have

set before thee life and death, blessing and cursing. Therefore choose life. . . . And the Lord said to Moses: Behold, thou shalt sleep with thy fathers; and this people will . . . go astray after the gods of the . . . land into which they go . . . and break my covenant which I have made with them. Then . . . I will forsake them, and I will hide my face from them, and they shall be devoured . . . so that they will say on that day, are these evils not come upon us, because our God is not among us? And I will surely hide my face on that day for all the evils which they shall have perpetrated. (Deuteronomy 30:15–20; 31:16–18)

This is a clear blueprint of Jewish history, in promise and realization. The terms of the covenant are repeated, again and again, throughout Scripture and rabbinic literature, and their fulfillment is historical record. The People that chose and was chosen to bear witness to the God who is revealed in the affairs of mankind cannot survive the betrayal of that God and the forcing Him to turn His face. We are given the choice to make God's presence large in the world of a man or to banish the *Shechinah,* but we cannot avoid the world. God's banishment paves the way to holocaust. In Jewish mysticism, every Jew is held to be an organic member of the corpus of the *Shechinah.* No people has flourished intact for very long in the eclipse of the divine; we Jews are left especially vulnerable – but we survive, and in our pain remain incandescent.

The Covenant's Truth Remains Eternal

There is an additional stipulation in the covenant with the Jewish people:

And it shall come to pass, when all these things are come upon thee . . . and thou shalt return to the Lord thy God and shalt obey his voice . . . with all thy heart and with all thy soul; that then the Lord thy God will turn thy captivity, and have compassion upon thee, and will return, and gather thee from all the nations among whom the Lord thy God has scattered thee (Deuteronomy 30:1–3).

That promise, too, echoes throughout the chronicles of God's dialogue with the Jewish people. The covenant is not for review, neither is the eternity of Jewish existence. God is in exile with His people, and when they permit Him, He returns from exile and is once more with the people. With Jewish justice and righteousness lies Jewish redemption. Until then, the door remains closed and the lights darkened.

The privilege of *being* a covenantal people is transcendent. The consequences of violation are agonizing. Many Jews have individually reasserted their allegiance to the collective covenant, even in bitter experience of its terms. I ask myself whether I should have the strength for such personal reassertion, had I endured them fully in my being. But I do know this: the covenant has unfolded for the people, and continues to unfold, in panlucid verity. It has not been broken by God, nor has He permitted the People to shake it off.

For the individual, the question of theodicy – the innocent who suffer, the evildoers who flourish – is ultimately the same whether suffering is in the midst of an inclusive catastrophe or in aloneness. The question to God – Why? – is the same for the first child struck down in human history and for the last to perish in Auschwitz. That is the eternal confrontation of all men with God.

R. Yohanan, the *amorah* who lost his children, would visit mourners and show a bone of his tenth, last son. A mute rendering of comfort in a sharing of faith: R. Yohanan remained the sage. Elisha ben Abuyah did not. Countless human beings, Jews and non-Jews, have found it possible, somehow, to take the way of Yohanan, Jews even after the German visitation. That is the challenge to the individual always. For the individual Jew to whom the evidence for the being of God as Judaism has known Him is too persuasive to elude, for all the suffering experienced, the seeking of new covenants is a search in the wrong dimension, a delusion.

In Response to David Weiss: A Covenant Shattered, A People Changed

The Hafetz Hayyim once said: "For the believer there are no questions, and for the unbeliever there are no answers."[2] David Weiss has sidestepped the questions posed by the Holocaust.

He has restated the eternity of the covenant that binds God and Israel, but he has not wrestled with the fundamental question: what can we say of that covenant in the wake of Auschwitz? Need we alter our understanding? Need we rely less on God and more on our fellow Jews in the struggle for survival? And finally, how can we talk of God's attributes of compassion and mercy in a world of death camps?

Weiss's conclusions are expected. *Bittachon* (trust), as Zwi Werblowski so beautifully demonstrated,[3] is central to the religious Jew's perception of the world. I concur that there are dangers in a Godless world. There is also a sense of emptiness and aloneness, a void. Jewish salvational history is jeopardized; most Jews do not live salvational history (except in its most secularized form of Israel and Zionism), and many devout Jews have politicized salvational history, identifying it with settlement of Judea and Samaria.

But in order to avoid the existential problem posed by the Holocaust, Professor Weiss is forced to deny the Holocaust's uniqueness and theological singularity. He also questions the religious integrity of unnamed thinkers who wrestle with the question of covenant after Auschwitz.

Space will not permit me to argue for the uniqueness of the Holocaust. I am uncomfortable with the term "Holocaust" – an *olah* (a sacrificial offering burned whole unto the Lord) – for I believe that the term softens and falsifies the impact of the event by imparting a religious meaning to the destruction. Yet the case for uniqueness is overwhelming. Divergent thinkers who disagree on many issues agree that the Holocaust was a singular and unprecedented event.

Its Uniqueness Should Not Be Denied

For Yehuda Bauer two historical elements mark the Holocaust as unique: the total planned annihilation of a people, and its quasi-religious-apocalyptic meaning. Forever an empiricist, Bauer argues that "to date, this has only happened to Jews."[4] Other thinkers maintain that the inner experience of the victim and the survivor or the mechanisms and processes of destruction mark the Holocaust as unique.

Suffice it to say that there is credible evidence advanced by distinguished scholars to suggest that the Holocaust was unprecedented not only in scope, setting, expectation, and proportion but in intention, intensity, duration, methodology, and consequences.

Weiss's reasons for denying the uniqueness and offending many by using the plural, small "h" (holocausts) is religious rather than scholarly. He is not alone. Many who object to the aesthetics or politics of Holocaust commemorations, or to the disproportionate role the Holocaust assumes in contemporary Jewish identity, strike out at the concept of uniqueness instead of tackling the troubling issue more directly.

Now to the heart of the matter: One good Midrash deserves another.

> Moses said: "The great, powerful, awesome God." Jeremiah came along and said: "Aliens are rampaging His Temple. Where is His awesomeness?" He no longer spoke [of God as] awesome. Daniel came along and said: "His children are slaves to foreigners. Where is His power?" He no longer spoke of God as powerful.[5]

The men of the Great Synod restored the crown to God's attributes by reinterpreting the power and awesomeness of God. This change took time. And although the words were the same, their meaning had changed.

The Covenant Has Been Reevaluated Before

Jewish history testifies to a reinterpretation of the covenant after every transformative historical experience: the Exodus, Sinai, the destruction of the first and second Temples, the defeat of 135 C.E. (Common Era), and the Spanish Inquisition. Although the covenant may be eternal, our understanding of the covenant and hence our relationship to the God of history was changed by each of these events.

When the great Jewish poet Jacob Gladstein said, "The Torah was given at Sinai and returned at Lublin," or when the novelist proclaims, "For the first time in Jewish history the covenant was broken . . . We must begin all over again . . ."[6] they are reshaping the language of tradition in order to bear witness to their historical experience. Perhaps until the next Great Synod we will be unable to speak of God's power or His mercy except in the most muted voices.

If we judge by the behavior of Jews as a people, our understanding of the covenant has changed. From Gush Emunim to Hashomer Hatzair, Jews have reentered history and are struggling for their survival by military and political means. They are no longer relying on the promise of God's salvation, nor are they content to await the Messiah. Even those who profess their faith in the eternal covenant have altered the way they behave in history.

Weiss does not refer to new covenantal thinkers by name. Nor can I recognize their thought from his characterizations. The men whose writings I have read share three essential convictions. First, the Holocaust has shattered the Jewish people and made it difficult to use religious language in a traditional way. Irving Greenberg's principle of truth sums it up best: "No statement, theological or otherwise, should be made that can not be said in the presence of the burning bodies of Jewish children."[7]

Second, they maintain that the Holocaust has imposed new responsibilities on the Jewish people. While I do not concur with Fackenheim's "commanding Voice of Auschwitz,"[8] he has captured the sense of obligation that the Holocaust has imposed upon the Jewish people.

Third, they are not closing the door on Judaism or on the Jewish witness "to something better."

With the notable exception of my teacher Richard Rubenstein, most post-Holocaust theologians believe that the reality of despair must energize us to hope. In a world of evil, we must create good. In a world without God, we must restore His image. This is neither an aberration nor a tragic path to assimilation. Rather, it is the essence of the contemporary Jewish challenge, the core of our witness.

For Weiss there are no questions. Many theologians of the Holocaust have chosen to wrestle with serious questions and not to avoid them or argue that they just don't exist. They have chosen to live with serious questions in a world of few answers.

5.   Issues in Teaching the Holocaust

In the decade of the 1970s, the teaching of the Holocaust in American universities increased 10,000 percent (from two courses in 1969 to two hundred in 1979). In the 1980s, the number has increased tenfold to two thousand courses. Nevertheless, there is little agreement on content or perspective. Whose history is to be taught: the perpetrator's, the victim's, or the bystander's? Neither is there consensus on where to begin the study of the Holocaust or when to conclude it (in terms of roots and repercussions). Should a course begin with religious leaders like the Apostle Paul or Martin Luther, with political antisemites or racists like Karl Lueger or Arthur Compte De Gobineau, with historical events like the Treaty of Versailles or Hitler's putsch? In this chapter I review the pedagogical controversies and suggest appropriate parameters for academic instruction.

Because of the nature of the subject, teachers of the Holocaust bear special burdens – moral, educational, and emotional. This chapter examines the many issues that shape Holocaust education.

The Holocaust was a watershed event in Western history, a paradigmatic manifestation of human evil intensified by the power of the state, fueled by technological and scientific accomplishment, and unchecked by moral, social, religious, or political constraints. The fact that the Holocaust was perpetrated not by an archaic, maniacal fringe but by the most cultured and scientifically advanced of Western societies presents us with a fundamental challenge. Whether restricted to the past ot a harbinger of the future, the Holocaust is a frightful indictment of contemporary existence. Slowly, the study of the Holocaust has made its way into academe as a legitimate field of research. In 1989, more than one thousand universities offered Holocaust courses within some twenty different departments in the humanities and social sciences.

The teacher of the Holocaust is beset by many difficulties, not the least of which is the restrictive nature of departmental divisions within the university. In what departmental context does the study of the Holocaust belong? In history, political science, government, economics, sociology, psychology, religion, philosophy, German literature, or Jewish studies? Courses on the Holocaust have occasioned a number of experiments at team teaching, with faculty often bridging not only departments but divisions within the university.

My own preference has been to offer the course as a collegewide seminar, an interdisciplinary program in the study of Western civilization, literature, history, and philosophy. By opting for the larger context of a university course and by cross-listing the course with another department, I guide the students' expectations and anticipate the diversity of material that will be presented. To teach a Holocaust course only within my home department of theology is to misrepresent the focus of the course.

Another consideration involves the perspective from which the topic is viewed. As with commemoration of the Holocaust, there are three histories that must be taught: those of the perpetrators, the victims, and the bystanders. The choice of histories dictates the books that are to be read and the fields to be covered. Raul Hilberg raises this question most directly in his introduction to *The Destruction of the European Jews* when he writes: "Lest one be misled by the word 'Jews' in the title, let it be pointed out that this is not a book about Jews. It is a book about the people who destroyed the Jews. Not much will be read here about the victims. The focus is placed on the perpetrators."[1]

The controversial aspects of Hilberg's book, those dimensions of his work that have caused acute discomfort to some Jewish historians who were angered by his portrayal of the Jews,[2] relate to Hilberg's determination to write a history of the perpetrators. Similarly, the curious omission of the murder of the Jews in concentration camps within Lucy Dawidowicz's *The War Against the Jews* can also be explained by her choice of histories. Dawidowicz's treatment of Jewish institutions within the ghetto, the Judenrat, the resistance, and the alternate community composed of self-help groups, is marked by her desire to treat autonomous Jewish institutions – functioning, of course, within extraordinarily narrow boundaries – none of which could exist in the context of total domination within the concentration camp. Thus, Dawidowicz's fidelity to her choice of historical focus leads her to neglect the concentration camp. Similarly, Martin Gilbert has chosen to compile a narrative history of the Holocaust from the perspective of the victims, with only an occasional reference to the perpetrators. Although his work is rich in detail and emotionally moving, he deliberately omits a larger framework of interpretation.

The perspective of the author also shapes the material that is presented. Again, the controversy can be clearly seen between Raul Hilberg and others. For Hilberg, fundamental questions concerning the Holocaust revolve around the governmental apparatus necessary to implement effectively so vast a state-sponsored enterprise: the bureaucratic functions, the legislative components, the economic details, and the interrelationship between competing segments of the German state. Dawidowicz, on the other hand, focuses her discussion on the ideological image of the Jew in the minds of Germans. Hitler occupies a central place within Dawidowicz's work, but he plays only a marginal role in Hilberg's discussion. For Uriel Tal and George Mosse, ideology plays a central role in the extermination of the Jews whereas bureaucracy and the state are tangential. For Rubenstein, Hilberg, and Arendt, the situation is reversed. The author's perspective determines what material he or she will evaluate and the lens that will be used in the process.

Kenneth Keniston's notion of objectivity in the social sciences is applicable to the study of the Holocaust. Keniston has argued that objectivity is achieved when the researcher reveals as fully and honestly as possible his own subjective perspective and thus allows the reader to compensate for this subjectivity. Objectivity is achieved in the interaction between the cautious, informed reader and the selected material.[3]

With respect to the Holocaust, I am convinced that most of these authors are correct in the material they consider; they are misleading when they extend the explanative power of their consideration beyond its natural boundary and when they claim exclusive legitimacy for their perspective. Oftentimes the task of the instructor is to clarify perspectives, to help the student perceive the value and limits of particular analyses and ultimately to broaden the students' perspective.

Language Clarification

Because language is the means by which we appropriate reality and create a universe of common discourse, the teacher of the Holocaust must be careful to understand the diverse and emotionally charged terminology that has marked Holocaust historiography. Nowhere is this difficulty more apparent than with regard to the question of resistance, which had been normatively defined as thwarting the enemy with violence. Yehuda Bauer suggested that the concept of resistance be expanded to include "any group action consciously taken in opposition to known or surmised laws, actions, or intentions directed against the Jews by the Germans and their supporters."[4]

In analyzing language and the reality it seeks to represent, two pitfalls must be avoided: mystification and simplification. The mystifiers claim that all Jews were martyrs while the simplifiers maintain that Jews went to their deaths like sheep to the slaughter. Such overstatements falsify history in an attempt to excuse or accuse.

Arthur A. Cohen's fiction may illumine some of the motivations disguised by historical discussions. In his ambitious and intriguing novel *In the Days of Simon Stern,* Cohen presents RATNER'S DECLARATION OF CONSCIENCE, which is signed in 1943 by Simon Stern, Cohen's failed messiah. Stern affirms:

> It does not matter whether Jews resist their enemies or submit, whether they fight back or remain passive, whether they claw or stamp their feet, whether they die nobly or abjectly or rain down curses, whether they sing songs or defecate in terror, whether they commit suicide or succumb to cardiac arrest.
>
> The fact is that more than two million are dead and many more will die.
>
> *The pride of the living may not be salvaged from the conduct of the dead.*[5]

In most discussions of resistance, the pride of the living is at stake, and the effort to salvage pride makes an evaluation of the conduct of the dead as reprehensible as it is impossible.

The only appropriate way out of the language quagmire is for the teacher to share with students the nature of the terms, along with their multiple uses and misuses, in order to reveal hidden agendas and presuppositions.

On a deeper level, there is profound reticence to confront Holocaust material. We are plagued by an acute, almost pornographic fascination with suffering and the infliction of pain. Those who have suffered have had an authentic experience and thus are peculiarly attractive to a generation seeking its own truths in a world of increasing fraud and deceitfulness. Similarly, many people are attracted to the Nazis and their power, to sadism and other forms of violence.

Even the morally and psychologically healthy student may face difficulties, as do scholars, in confronting the Holocaust and its terrifying implications. In a masterful essay, Lawrence Langer has posed the dilemma most poignantly:

> The implications reach far beyond moral ideology to the role of time and history in human destiny, to the structure of character and the very unity of our lives in the twentieth century. History assures us that man is superior to time when retrospectively he can explain the unexpected, account, in this instance, for the extermination of a people, uncover a system for surviving and thus reduce the event to a partial intellectual order that somehow theoretically balances the price in human lives paid for that order. But from the perspective of the victims, who of course far outnumbered the survivors, the disorder of meaningless death contradicts the ordering impulses of time. Those who died for nothing during the Holocaust left the living with the paralyzing dilemma of facing a perpetually present grief. To the puzzled inquiry why interest in the Holocaust seems to grow as the event recedes into the past, one answer may be that there is no inner space or time to bury it in.[6]

Langer dissents from the attempt of Viktor Frankl and Terrence Des Pres to impose moral order and triumph on Holocaust survivors. He continually argues that the experiences in the camps, the choiceless choices of the victims, undermine our collective universe, which is predicated on a sense of human dignity that demands certain external supports. In the morally denuding atmosphere of death camps, a system of meaning evaporates. Rather than confront the void, values derived from a pre-Holocaust universe are imposed. However, to introduce students to the world of Auschwitz is to shatter illusions, undermine values, and restrain faith in humanity. Human life comes to be seen as precarious; social institutions appear vulnerable. Certainly, we are all reluctant to face this phenomenon, yet an honest confrontation is morally necessary if we are to be faithful to our task.

By interweaving history with biography, secondary sources with primary sources, a balance can be struck between the vast depersonalization of the Holocaust history and individual stories. Diaries and memoirs, novels and oral histories should be read along with standard works in the field. The student thus gains richer insight into the changing circumstances of victims, the conditions within the ghettos and camps, and the monumental sense of loss. Personal accounts concretize historical discussion while fortifying student interest as well as the discipline required to tackle extensive reading.

The content of a Holocaust course is difficult to delineate. Where should the study begin and end? Readings could start with the Gospel accounts of the Crucifixion or the loss of Jerusalem in the year 70 C.E., or with the origins in slavery of the Jewish people.[7] Jewish existence in the diaspora must be traced. Extermination and Jewish victimization predominate, yet the world that was lost in its diversity must also be presented. A romantic view of Eastern Europe will not suffice; the forces that threatened that world (both internal and external) must also be examined. The bystander, as well as the victim and perpetrator, needs to be portrayed. Finally, the Holocaust's implications for Judaism and Christianity are unavoidable.

One must beware that the Holocaust does not become a new threshold for evil or that students become insensitive to lesser tragedies. (Witness, for example, the treatment of the Holocaust by some neo-Nazi movements that concede that 1 million or 1.5 million Jews were killed but reject the higher figure as if the 1 million murdered were acceptable.) Neither should the Holocaust be superimposed on disproportionate events; the Jewish community errs when it compares acts of terrorism or antisemitism to the Holocaust. In addressing questions about God's presence or absence at Auschwitz or about the viability of tradition after the Holocaust, a dialectic tension is often maintained. The teacher should present rather than resolve these questions for students. Unlike Wiesel, I believe that a teacher of the Holocaust must begin with the assumption that the story of the Holocaust can be understood even by those who were not there. If, in the end, a measure of comprehension eludes us – as it inevitably will – so be it. The limits of knowledge will be encountered in the end, but they should not paralyze us at the beginning. As Hannah Arendt wrote in the introduction to *The Origins of Totalitarianism:*

> Comprehension does not mean denying the outrageous, deducing the unprecedented from the precedence or explaining phenomena by such analogies and generalities that the impact of reality and the shock of experience are no longer felt. It means, rather, having and bearing consciously the burden which our century has placed upon us – neither denying its existence nor submitting meekly to its weight. Comprehension, in short, means the unpremeditated, attentive facing up to, and resisting of, reality – whatever it may be.[8]

6. What We Should Teach Our Children

What are we to tell children about the murder of Jewish children? How do we teach trust in a dangerous world? Will sharing the story of this terrible tragedy frighten our children? Are we bequeathing to them a burden too great to bear?

This chapter asks painful and personal questions. It urges that the magnitude of evil in the Holocaust be communicated truthfully to our children at appropriate ages. Silence and denial only create more problems; falsification invites greater distrust.

As I noted in Chapter 4, Irving Greenberg has argued that no statement, theological or otherwise, should be made that could not be credible in the presence of burning children. What, then, should be said to living children about the world of burning children? We run major risks in telling children anything about the Holocaust. Yet if we do not tell them about it, we may be communicating something even more significant. (Witness the problem experienced by children of survivors whose parents have shrouded their past in silence.) To tell youngsters about the Holocaust is to challenge their sense of security in the world, to increase their suspicions about the enterprise of socialization and education, and to burden them with baggage we may be unable to lighten. We are caught on the horns of a dilemma from which there is not easy extrication.

Perhaps we have moved too quickly; perhaps we have begun by asking the wrong questions or by asking the right questions prematurely. American Jews are prone to live vicariously through their children, to ask the question: "what should we tell our children?" before confronting what we should tell ourselves. Let us therefore ask the preliminary question: what must we confront regarding the Holocaust?

I believe that the Holocaust is one of those few events that forever transforms the nature of what it means to be human. By its scope, nature, and magnitude, the Holocaust alters our understanding of culture and existence. An unspoken premise of the advocates of culture and education is that the refinements of art and learning make us into better people and intensify our moral worth. Yet the Holocaust was perpetrated not by the least sophisticated of nations but by the most advanced. Furthermore, the elements within the society that proved capable of such heinous deeds came from all spectrums of society including philosophers and scientists, musicians and engineers, lawyers and ministers, artists and intellectuals. No segment of German society proved immune.

The destruction of the Jews became the collective enterprise of Nazi Germany, its most basic goal. The Holocaust marks the "perfection" of the destructive process. The Holocaust was a systematic, unrelenting series of acts undertaken by the state as a central policy. As the system "improved," the killers were no longer sent after the victims; instead, the victims were brought to the killers and exterminated "cleanly" and efficiently at low cost. Much of what we understood about modernity and humanity must now be reunderstood. We now know that people could love good music and kill young children. They could be admirable husbands and concerned fathers yet spend their days in constant contact with death and destruction. Society can be organized in such a way that the enterprise of death becomes triumphant. All this is possible in the twentieth century with technology facilitating the process.

The loss in the Holocaust is overwhelming. One out of three of the world's Jews was killed. Eighty percent of all Jewish scholars and rabbis perished. A common universe of humanity did not bind the killer to the killed. All institutions failed. Jews were betrayed by their trust – in the goodness of people, the power of God, the moral commitments of nations, and the wisdom of their own leadership. We must now confront not merely the failure of Western civilization but the vulnerability of Jewish existence as well.

The Jewish community has responded to the Holocaust, perhaps without profundity, perhaps with a lack of articulated clarity, and perhaps without sufficient direction, but it has responded in basic ways. American Jewry's central concern with the survival of the state of Israel involves the realization that powerlessness and homelessness left Jews defenseless. Finally, Jews have managed to create in the wake of death. They have become more militant in their advocacy of Jewish rights and concerns, more willing to confront governments and other sources of power to advance Jewish causes. Jewish culture has experienced a sense of resurgence and rebirth.

Teach the Holocaust's Lessons Directly

What should we tell our children of this reality and of our response? The first answer is stark and brief. The truth must be told. The horror of the Holocaust cannot be sweetened or avoided. It need not be dwelled on for its own sake, but if we avoid speaking about it, we run the risk of distorting the event and giving our children a false sense of what grieves us. To live authentically as a Jew today, one must be aware of the reality of evil and its startling triumphs.

We must also tell our children of their own preciousness. If a million children could be exterminated, then the importance of the new generation is intensified. We know both the meaning of loss and the beauty of blessing. Every child is a triumph over the void; the birth of every child is an affirmation of possibility and hope in a world desperately in need of both. If our children know this about themselves and about our attitude toward them, perhaps the insecurity they are bound to feel in the face of the Holocaust can be mediated.

We must also tell our children about the nature of authority and the limits of education. Authority must not be trusted blindly; we must teach our children a healthy skepticism toward all forms of authority. Our children should be taught to trust their own perceptions and be sensitive to the arbitrary nature of authority. Authority should be challenged in the name of justice, condemned when wrong and praised when correct.

Concerning relationships with non-Jews, distinctions must be made. A delicate balance should be struck. Gone are the days when we should tell our children that behind every non-Jew lurks the shadow of antisemitism or that the whole world is against us. Neither can we deny the reality of hatred and isolation. Jewish children must know of the fundamental conflicts between Judaism and forms of Christianity that have not confronted the teaching of contempt toward Jews within Christian tradition.

As to Jewish identity, the next generation should not remain Jewish *because* of the Holocaust, nor should they live a Jewish life that is unaffected by the Holocaust. The Holocaust teaches that all people do not live "happily ever after." For Jews, the Exodus must be reunderstood after Auschwitz and Revelation beside the deafening silence of God.

Finally, we have a particular obligation to teach our children about suffering. We must teach our children, by example and by deed, that suffering is not the key to greatness or accomplishment, that suffering confers no honors; suffering yields no virtue. Suffering does demand confrontation and, above all, alleviation. To ennoble suffering is to condone it in some measure. Suffering must not be rationalized.

The Holocaust resists answers and raises significant questions. We must share our questions with our children and introduce them to a world that resists answers. Questions can be pursued together.

7.   The Shadows of the Holocaust

In the period between the 1967 Six Day War and the 1982 War in Lebanon, world Jewry told a simple story about the implications of the Holocaust. In short, powerlessness invites victimization; therefore, the Jewish people must assume power and engage history as actors rather than victims. The memories of victimization should sensitize the newly empowered community to the urgency of its task, its limits, and its risks.

In the years since the debacle of Lebanon, the legacy of the Holocaust is more complex, more troubled. After the intifada, *the lessons of the Holocaust are no less relevant, but the applications seem more illusory. This chapter probes the implications of the Holocaust for a generation that has experienced the joy of Jerusalem's reunification and the pain of occupation. In the aftermath of Israel's greatest victory, it stands at a moral crossroads.*

In order to avoid confronting the full implications of the Holocaust, Jews often make the mistake of focusing exclusively on antisemitism. For religious Jews, this approach offers the dubious solace of sidestepping the theological problems raised by the Holocaust. By presuming continuity, the event must be understood within traditional solutions to the problem of evil. Some religious Jews fear that the importance of the Holocaust will be intensified – and even overemphasized – if it cannot be contained within the categories of Jewish history.

As we have seen, the Holocaust differs from previous manifestations of antisemitism in that earlier expressions were episodic, geographically limited, illegal (they took place outside the law), and religiously rather than biologically based. Jews were killed for what they believed or practiced; conversion and emigration were possible.

By contrast, Nazism was unrelenting; for twelve years the destruction of the Jewish people was a German priority. Trains that could have been used to carry soldiers to the front or transport injured personnel to the rear were diverted to bring Jews to their death. The persecution of Jews was geographically widespread throughout Europe, from Central Russia to the Spanish border. Furthermore, the extermination of Jews was conducted legally. The legal system served as an instrument of oppression. In fact, it has been argued that the Nazis committed "no crime"[1] in that the persecution of Jews and their annihilation was a policy of state, utilizing all facets of the government. Most important, Jews were killed not for *what* they were, for what they practiced or believed, but for the *fact* that they were. All Jews were to be exterminated, not merely the Jewish soul. Jews were no longer considered, as they had been in Christian theology, the symbol of evil; rather, they had become its embodiment and as such were to be murdered. Raul Hilberg has written, "The missionaries of Christianity had said in effect: 'You have no right to live among us as Jews.' The secular rulers who followed had proclaimed: 'You have no right to live among us.' The German Nazis at last decreed: 'You have no right to live.' "[2] Unlike Christianity, the Third Reich had no need for Jews to witness its anticipated triumph.

In most cases, Jews had few choices regarding their fate; therefore, the traditional category of martyrdom does not accurately apply to victims of the Holocaust who died not because of their beliefs but because of their births as descendants of Jewish grandparents. Saul Esh struggled to develop a new category of martyrdom, suggesting that the sanctification of the Name, *Kiddush hashem,* was not applicable in the Holocaust.

This is a time for *kiddush ha-hayyim,*the sanctification of life, and not for *kiddush ha-Shem,* the holiness of martyrdom. Previously, the Jew's enemy sought his soul and the Jew sanctified his body in martyrdom [i.e., he made a point of preserving what the enemy wished to take from him]; now the oppressor demands the Jew's body and the Jew is obliged therefore to defend it, to preserve his life.[3]

Lawrence Langer dissents. His suggestion in *Versions of Survival* "that we consider the event from the perspective of the *victims* who far outnumbered the survivors" alludes to the fact that another way of softening the blow of the Holocaust is to speak of survivors and martyrs – but never victims.

Demonic and Bureaucratic Evil

The Nazi policy of extermination involved all levels of German society. We deceive ourselves if we imagine that Nazism was a demonic fringe group within German society. In fact, Nazis were drawn from the society as a whole. For example, the Einsatzgruppen – the men who ran the mobile killing units that rounded up and murdered Jews – were composed not of German criminals but of ordinary citizens.

> The great majority of the officers of the *Einsatzgruppen* were professional men. As we look over their files we discover among them a physician, a professional opera singer, and a large number of lawyers. These men were in no sense hoodlums, delinquents, common criminals, or sex maniacs; most were intellectuals, most were educated at the universities. By and large, they were in their thirties, and undoubtedly they wanted a certain measure of power, fame, and success. However, there is no indication that any of them sought an assignment to a Kommando. All we know is that they brought to their new tasks all the skills and training which, as men of thought, they were capable of contributing. These men, in short, became efficient killers.[4]

Not only were the killers drawn from a cross section of German society, the entire apparatus of German bureaucracy was marshaled for the task. The churches and the Health Ministry supplied birth records to define and isolate Jews while the post office delivered statements of definition, expropriation, denaturalization, and deportation. The Economic Ministry confiscated Jewish wealth and property; the universities denied Jewish students admission and degrees while dismissing Jewish faculty;[5] German industry fired Jewish workers, officers, and board members, disenfranchising Jewish stockholders; and government travel bureaus coordinated the schedule and billing procedures for the railroads that carried Jews to their death.

Efficiency in Extermination

The process of extermination itself was bureaucratically systematic. Following the mob destruction of *Kristallnacht* – a pogrom that occurred in November 1938 in which at least 236 Jews were killed, 20,000 arrested, thousands of Jewish businesses looted and burned, and 1,100 synagogues destroyed or damaged – random acts of violence were replaced by organized, relatively passionless operations. Similarly, the angry, riotous actions of the S.A. gave way to the disciplined, professional procedures of the S.S., which by 1942 had substituted massive impersonal factories of extermination for the earlier mobile killing units. The location and operation of the camps were based on calculations of accessibility and cost-effectiveness, the trademarks of modern business practice. German corporations actually profited from the industry of death. Pharmaceutical firms, unrestrained by fear of side effects, tested drugs on camp inmates, and companies competed for contracts to build ovens or supply gas for extermination. (Indeed, industry was even concerned with protecting the patents for its products.) German engineers working for Topf and Sons supplied one camp alone with forty-six ovens capable of burning five hundred bodies an hour.[6]

Adjacent to the extermination camp at Auschwitz was a privately owned, corporately sponsored concentration camp called I.G. Auschwitz, a division of I.G. Farben. This multidimensional petrochemical complex brought human slavery to its ultimate "perfection" by reducing human beings to consumable raw materials from which all mineral life was systematically drained before the bodies were recycled into the Nazi war economy: gold teeth for the treasury, hair for mattresses, ashes for fertilizer. In a relentless search for the least expensive and most efficient means of extermination, German scientists experimented with a variety of gases until they discovered the insecticide Zyklon B, which could kill 2,000 persons in less than thirty minutes. The same type of

ingenuity and control that facilitates modern industrial development was rationally applied to the process of destruction.

The total abrogation of human rights and the destruction of an
entire people in the Holocaust must be seen for what it was –
not a reversion to barbarism but a thoroughly modern operation,
utilizing the most advanced procedures of bureaucratic organization, industrial management, scientific achievement, and technological sophistication. Furthermore, the Holocaust reflects in the
extreme some of the basic tendencies within Western society –
whether demographic, political, or religious. The Holocaust reflects in excess social tendencies that are fundamentally modern.[7]

Demographically, for three hundred years Western civilization
produced people who were superfluous to society, people who
could not find an appropriate place within the economic mainstream. For most of that period there was a safety valve for this
population; they could be sent either to settle the New World or
to colonize Africa and Asia, transporting back to their homeland
the major fruits of that colonization.[8]

American Jews, like numerous other immigrants to the New
World, are descendants of a superfluous population; the first generation of these Eastern European immigrants felt that there was
little future for them in Europe and were therefore willing to forsake their homeland in order to settle in America. They abandoned
family and friends, language and tradition, in search of a more
promising future. However, once the New World was no longer
able to absorb the residue from the Old, a dilemma arose. If society cannot ship out excess people and if it cannot absorb them
within the economy, the next logical step is to send them up in
smoke. Needless to say, the logical solution need not be a moral
or desirable one, yet the wish to reduce a population was part of
the rationale of destruction. Hitler spoke in terms of *Lebensraum,*
or living space.

Superfluous population, or the need for greater living space, is
not merely a problem of the past but a future threat as well. When
40 percent of the black teenage population in America is unem-
ployed within a society whose production is not labor intensive,
a surplus population problem is in evidence. (When a society contains superfluous people, it may choose – for political, racial, or

religious reasons – to eliminate *any* group, not necessarily the people least needed at the time. A shift in economic roles can follow later.)

The young are not the most significant of our superfluous populations. The old are both encouraged and compelled by law to cease contributing to society, and due to the rapid advance of knowledge and mobility, the old frequently lose their roles as repositories of wisdom for younger generations.[9] We have generally lost the extended family of former times. We send older people off to old-age homes or to the Sun Belt adult housing projects away from family and community. It is no wonder that Governor Richard Lamm of Colorado began to speak in our society of "the right time to die."

What allowed for the destruction of the Jews and for the choice of Jews as victims is not merely that they were targeted to relieve a problem of superfluous population, but that they also occupied those positions within the society to which others aspired. Eliminating Jews made room for people who would otherwise have been in danger of becoming superfluous. Demographic tendencies did not operate alone; alongside them were religious propensities. A history of severe persecution, murder, and expulsion was Christian in origin, yet only in the twentieth century – in a time of increased secularization – were expulsion and forced conversion escalated to outright extermination. Before the twentieth century, religious barriers prohibited the wholesale destruction of the Jewish people. There were theological battles, with strong psychological overtones, concerning who was the chosen of God or which religious community possessed the truth. Jews were accused of rejecting Jesus as the Christ and of killing the savior, but only in the secularized twentieth century was a final solution contemplated and implemented. Indeed, part of the anger directed at the Nazis was not at their goal of eliminating the Jews but merely at the means of elimination they chose.

In addition to the demographic and religious tendencies that climaxed in the Holocaust, the growth of bureaucracy politically triumphed. Within a bureaucratic structure, wild and random acts of violence were replaced by a system of depersonalized terror. At virtually each stage of the destruction process, the killing became distant, abstract, and efficient. The task of the bureaucrat is to do his duty without bias and scorn, without the recognition of the individual as a person. Raul Hilberg has pointed out that no disorder was tolerated by the S.S. Orgies, personal cruelty, loose behavior, or random violence were abuses of the machine and were not tolerated unless authorized. Authorization for such activities was not difficult to obtain, but unauthorized behavior was punished.[10]

If we live in a world where, in the words of Victor Frankl, "the unimaginable has happened, where the reality of evil has surpassed the imagination's capacity to deal with it,"[11] and where the destructive process is a fundamental expression of our civilization, then we are forced to transform our understanding of humanity. Our basic religious understanding of man and God has been shattered, and we must somehow replace these images and begin what Emil Fackenheim has called "mending the world," recalling the term *tikkun* that was central to post–Spanish Inquisition theology.[12] The perception of human rights and the human condition has been altered; we now see the universe through a prism of despair. One can become skeptical, discouraged by the devaluation of human rights while, at the same time, energized by a greater urgency to reaffirm human values.

The Holocaust as Temptation

Unfortunately, the Holocaust may serve as an example: a temptation, a precedent. Hundreds of thousands died in Thailand and Cambodia, victims of an auto-genocide inflicted by one people upon their own. Initially, the Cambodians died of starvation, a passive program of murder that was identical to the first stage in the extermination of European Jewry. The Nazis employed starvation to decimate the population of the Ukraine in the harsh winter of 1942. Rubenstein has called starvation "clean violence."[13] So lethal was the power of disease and starvation in the Warsaw Ghetto that life could not have been sustained for twenty years. Yet the Nazis were unwilling to wait. In testimony given before the Senate Judiciary Committee in 1979, Senator Jack Danforth mentioned that within Cambodia there were persistent rumors of gassings. Precedent invites repetition, if not in reality then at least in imagination.

Power and Survival

There are specifically Jewish lessons to be learned from the Holocaust, some of which have already become the cornerstone of Jewish consciousness: lessons of solidarity, commitment, power, and risk. In the aftermath of World War I, many Jews sought international guarantees for Jewish rights as part of the larger question of minority rights within majority cultures. After World War II, the Jewish people in overwhelming numbers became Zionists; that is, they understood that Jewish rights could not be guaranteed without power and sovereignty, without an army and a state. After the Holocaust, Jews learned that powerlessness is no virtue because powerlessness invites victimization.

Power must be shared and spread if human rights and dignity are to be preserved; an imbalance of power invites its total exercise. As Irving Greenberg has said, Jewish powerlessness only helps the antisemite. Powerlessness on the part of any minority aids would-be oppressors.[14]

However, the shadows of past and present politics have confused contemporary discussions of Jewish power. Rabbinic Judaism was restrained in its discussions of power, especially after the failure of the Bar-Kokhba revolt in 132–35 C.E. Rabbinic Judaism spiritualized the military triumph of the Maccabees and shaped the Passover *Hagaddah,* which transformed the story of redemption from Egypt into a quietistic tale that minimized the human role in redemption. For example, the name Moses never appears in the *Hagaddah;* God alone is credited with redemption.

As contemporary Jews sought sovereignty and scanned their history for a tradition of power, they returned to the biblical era, with its warrior kings, and the revolts against Rome to counterbalance Jewish powerlessness during the Holocaust. David Biale has demonstrated the fallacy of contemporary Israelis who evoke a heroic military past of independence during the First and Second Commonwealths, as well as of religious Jews who read recent Jewish powerlessness back into all Jewish history. Those who view history through the lens of either extreme power or power-lessness are forced to misread the past and hence mislead Jews regarding their future.

Power and Its Limits

Like all resources, power is limited and so must be used wisely in order to gain maximum impact. Jews run the risk of misapplying power, of overestimating it and thus expending it inadequately or incorrectly. Jews are not as powerful as antisemites depict or as Jews would imagine in moments of grandeur. Nor are Jews as powerless as they portray themselves in a post-Holocaust world when feeling oppressed and beleaguered is considered proof of virtue. Biale writes:

> From biblical times to the present day, Jews have wandered the uncertain terrain between power and powerlessness, never quite achieving the power necessary to guarantee long-term security, but equally avoiding, with a number of disastrous exceptions, the abyss of absolute impotence. They developed the consummate skill of living with uncertainty and insecurity.[15]

Past as Metaphor

Yehoshafat Harkabi, a former chief of Israel's military intelligence and professor of political science at the Hebrew University, concurs with Biale that contemporary Jews are often confused about the role of power in their past. In his controversial Israeli best seller *The Bar-Kokhba Syndrome: Risk and Realism in International Politics*, Harkabi argues that a mythologization of the past prevents realistic policies in the present and can spell catastrophe. Harkabi explores three great tragedies of ancient Jewish history: the destruction of the first Temple in 586 B.C.E., the second Temple in 70 C.E., and the Bar-Kokhba revolt of 132–35 C.E.

During the waning days of the first Temple, Jeremiah preached a politics of compromise with Babylonia, asserting that national unity was no guarantee of victory against so mighty an enemy.

Six centuries later, Yochanan ben Zakkai recognized the futility of war against Rome and, like Jeremiah, counseled nonconfrontation and accommodation. Zealotry again clouded political perceptions when Bar-Kokhba and his followers revolted against Rome, a policy that ended in total defeat. Harkabi cautions against the twin tendencies of contemporary Jews to treat history as beyond human influence or as totally subject to willful manipulation.

There is a temptation – especially now – to romanticize Jewish successes in battle without a balanced awareness of past military catastrophes. Some Jews are overly reliant on divine intervention, while others confuse the limits of power with the degree of collective determination. Past defeats are wrongly attributed to Jewish disunity rather than to the enemy's strength. If the past is a metaphor for the present, Harkabi's message is clear: Jews dare not evade the exercise of power, but they must accurately assess the limits of power. In an interdependent world, the risk of confrontation must be weighed against the value of accommodation.

The Fear of Powerlessness

Power does not offer absolute security. As we see in Israel today, power has not eliminated Jewish vulnerability. In fact, an empowered Israel, which is the dominant presence in the Middle East, cannot escape a sense that its basic existence is threatened. The Jewish people in the diaspora cannot easily accept the reality of Israel's power and continue to see even self-proclaimed wars of choice as battles for survival.

Much to Israel's dismay, in both the War in Lebanon and the stuggle on the West Bank, Jews have discovered that power enables the formerly oppressed to become oppressors. The fear of powerlessness and a persistent sense of vulnerability – real and imagined – is not easily erased even when the formerly powerless gain significant power.

Furthermore, the long-term impact of powerlessness has been to cement a feeling of victimization among some Jews, who cannot recognize the changed circumstances of contemporary Jews both in Israel and in the United States. Because Jews have been victimized for so long, they feel immune to the pressure of public opinion or the conventions of the Western world and free to behave as they see fit without recognizing the responsibilities of an empowered people. A powerless minority people agitating for its basic survival is in a rather different situation than is an empowered majority community that should respect the rights of the minority. In part, some Israelis and their American Jewish supporters fail to appreciate how far the Jewish people have come over the past generation. [16]

Solidarity

Powerlessness and antisemitism were not the only factors that led to past Jewish victimization. During the Holocaust, an absence of solidarity and an unwillingness to risk tentative acceptance in America for Jews overseas further endangered European Jewry. So frightened were American Jews of the label "Jewish war" that Jews were unable to defend their people's interests, even when it became clear that the Nazis were waging a second war against the Jews. Jewish leaders were compliant when confronted with the argument that special interests must be subservient to the general war effort. Such reasoning often took lethal forms. Witness the exchange of correspondence in which American Jewish leaders were informed that a diversion of American forces would be required if Auschwitz were to be bombed, a diversion that could not be justified since it might provoke "even more vindictive action on the part of the Germans."[17] This letter, signed by John J. McCloy, was sent to the World Jewish Congress in August 1944, when 20,000 Jews a day were being murdered at Auschwitz. "More vindictive action" would be virtually impossible.

The charges and countercharges, the writing and rewriting of history, are still extremely divisive for American Jews. In 1983, a commission chaired by former justice Arthur Goldberg tried to evaluate the historical record. Within weeks, the project was mired in controversy, and the final report – an odd collection of essays and responses – could not achieve consensus among its authors.

Jewish Unity: Its Virtues and Perils

Timidity in pursuit of Jewish interests has been rejected. So, too, has disunity and dissent. If the principal sin of a previous generation was religious heresy, the fundamental heresy of this generation – the one that leads to bureaucratic excommunication – is dissent from the policies of the state of Israel.

In the aftermath of the Holocaust, Jews have insisted on solidarity. Perhaps the monumental accomplishment of American Jewry in the postwar years has been its sense of connection with fellow Jews, its willingness to assume their burdens. Most recently, this commitment has been powerfully expressed in relationship to Soviet Jewry, where the cause demands sustained effort including political pressure in Washington and around the world, publicity for refusenik families, significant funds for resettlement in Israel and the United States, and an infrastructure to accommodate thousands of refugees in Europe awaiting resettlement. American Jews marched in Washington on the eve of the 1987 Reagan–Gorbachev summit. Two hundred and fifty thousand demonstrators came (almost 4 percent of the entire American Jewish community) to underscore the importance of the Soviet Jewry issue despite fears that it would appear self-centered or detrimental to the Intermediate-Range Nuclear Forces (INF) treaty. Likewise, American Jews have become increasingly combative against politicians who criticize Israel. They are willing to flex their political muscle with respect to specifically Jewish concerns.

"We are One" is the banner of the United Jewish Appeal, which substitutes the proclamation of the unity of the Jewish people for the biblical proclamation of God's unity ("Hear, oh Israel, the Lord Our God, the Lord is one"). By political activities, demonstrations, and acts of protest, American Jews have become activists, demanding community. They have chosen not to replicate the passivity attributed to American Jews during the Holocaust.

Yet unity, too, has its costs and perils. As Harkabi has reminded us, the wrong political vision does not necessarily become right through national consensus. Audacity as a temporary tactic cannot be substituted for a long-range strategy.

The Legacy of the Holocaust

All too often, every crisis or enemy in Jewish life is measured against the shadow of the Holocaust. Jews must be wary lest they become insensitive to other forms of evil that are less devastating.

We can also come to feel that suffering confers privilege, that it is a guarantor of virtue.

There is also a danger that Jews may come to view everything as a Holocaust, as Holocaust-like. If everything is a holocaust, then nothing is The Holocaust. (Note the current use of the term "holocaust" without the prefix *the,* implying that "holocaust" is a condition rather than a specific, unprecedented historical event.) In order to preserve the meaning of the word and its importance, we must use it restrictively.

The Holocaust may also cause us to misperceive phenomena that must be confronted from a different perspective. Yasir Arafat may be dangerous and destructive, but – contrary to the popular Jewish imagination – he is not Hitler. And the pre-1967 borders of Israel may be difficult and cumbersome, without strategic depth and highlands, but they are not (to use Deputy Foreign Minister Benjamin Netanyahu's words) "the borders of Auschwitz."[18] The stones thrown by Palestinian youths angered by Israel's presence are potentially lethal, but they are not synonymous with the Nazi assault against powerless Jewish civilians.

What is the legacy of the Holocaust that contemporary Jews bring to the struggle for human rights? First of all, there is the memory of abuse, the knowledge that often, when human rights and human dignity are threatened, Jews are the first victims but not the last. The Nazis killed millions of other people from many nations in a process originally designed for the destruction of Jews. (The mechanisms of Jewish destruction were first suggested for the murder of those Germans who were an embarrassment to the myth of Aryan supremacy – the mentally and physically retarded or the emotionally ill.)

Jews continue to maintain a sense of identity with victims. (*New Republic* journalist Michael Kinsley once explained the Jewish vote for Walter Mondale: "Jews live like Episcopalians and vote like Puerto Ricans.") Some neoconservative leaders have argued that Jews seem willing to sacrifice their own interests in pursuit of universal justice, but the charge seems vacuous in light of the enormous energies Jews dedicate to specifically Jewish causes.

Another resource in the struggle for human rights is a willingness to take risks. Having seen how Soviet Jews gambled with their lives in the name of an unknown future, free Jews have gained courage. Jewish tradition speaks of the Exodus with the central symbol of the *matzah,* the bread of poverty. With regard to freedom and human dignity, Jews must be prepared to go into the desert without waiting for bread to rise. An unwillingness to leave a secure, material environment imperils Argentinean, South African, and Iranian Jewry, intensifying the global responsibilities of free-world Jewish communities.

Jewish tradition, particularly the notion of one God for all people, gave the world the essential concept that the human community is interrelated. When the rabbis spoke of the right of a human being irrespective of status or stature, they used the term *nivrah betzelem* (created in the divine image), thus inspiring equality and sanctity. In the delicate balance between the exercise of power and its restraint, in conformity with our creaturely status, human rights are born.

Projections for the Future

The liberal tradition of Jews has been challenged in recent years by the collapse of universalist dreams, displays of antisemitism on the part of minorities at home and abroad, and sustained military conflict in the Mideast. In Israel, the reality of Jewish sovereignty has challenged the traditional identification of Jews with minority rights. The battle for Israel's survival will not be decided solely on military or political grounds; a spiritual issue is also at stake. How does a country remain secure, democratic, and Jewish in character while ruling over a minority population that may soon outnumber it? The question Israel faces is Nietzschean: Is Judaism the religion of the powerless, or does it also have something to say to those with power?[19] How does one struggle to retain crucial freedom of action while avoiding an indecent ethic of triumphalism or chauvinism?

After each historical shift in the condition of the Jewish people, Jews have transformed their understanding of chosenness and redemption. The contemporary redefinition of these concepts may shape the politics of Israel and the content of American Judaism.

There are two disparate images of the messiah in Jewish history. One vision portrays the messianic period as an abrupt end to history; the other conception, born after the Spanish Inquisition, involves a prolonged struggle to reunify divine sparks scattered by the cosmic catastrophe of creation. In Israel and America, there are Jews who believe that the world now hovers on the brink of the apocalypse. Some Christians and Muslims share this sense of an imminent transformation, an expectancy that tramples ordinary values and liberty. Against this position stands a more moderate principle of redemption, which maintains the struggle for human rights and dignity as an enduring challenge.

Part II   Jewish Thought and Modern History

8. Franz Rosenzweig and Martin Buber Reconsidered

The first half of this book probed the implications of the Holocaust for contemporary Jewish life. The next part will deal with Jewish faith. The following chapter interprets the writings of Martin Buber and Franz Rosenzweig insofar as they engage the role of ritual, norms, and law in the religious life of the non-Orthodox Jew. The relationship between form and content will involve the problems of fidelity and faith, descipline and spontaneity, experience and revelation.

For the past several years I have been teaching a course in modern Jewish thought. As I approached the material with my students, we read both the original sources and the critical essays on the designated thinkers. Each time I taught the material my students were surprised by the acclaim accorded by Jewish writers to the work of Frank Rosenzweig and the severe criticism directed toward Martin Buber. The students' estimation of the relative importance of both men reinforced my own conviction that the works of these philosophers require reconsideration.

Rosenzweig's conception of the role of the Jewish people in history is hopeless and dangerously outdated, and his current theological importance rests mainly on his personal stance toward *halakhah* (Jewish law) and his return to Judaism. In an era that has experienced the erosion of normative structures (the state, the family, the synagogue, the school) or at least the irrelevance of such structures for many people, Martin Buber's much criticized non-nomistic position on Jewish law may have increasing significance. Finally, the debate between Rosenzweig and Buber on Jewish law and, in reality, on the whole concept of structured, normative existence, is being carried on today by the non-Orthodox Jewish community as it struggles with its Jewishness in the aftermath of anomie.

Buber, Rosenzweig, and American Jews

Just after the death of Martin Buber in June 1965, Chaim Potok –
then a young, little-known academic – published a critical essay
on "Martin Buber and the Jews."[1] In this article Potok wrote of
the bitter irony that Buber, the philosopher of dialogue who is
most honored by non-Jews as an authentic representative of Jewish teaching, is "today virtually incapable of entering into dialogue
with his own people."[2] According to Potok, Buber's work was
regarded with great suspicion by Orthodox Jews for its anomic
quality, by Conservative and Reform Jews for its mysticism, by
Israelis for his involvement with *Ichud* (a Jewish and Arab political
group that advocated a binational state of Jews and Arabs), by
scholars of Judaism for the serious flaws in the treatment of Hasidism, by secularists for the religious focus, and by some Jews for
Buber's closeness to Jesus of Nazareth (as distinct from the Christ
of Christian faith).

In that same article, Potok spoke positively about the attraction
of Franz Rosenzweig. "Those who were inclined toward existen-
tialism find they have more in common with Franz Rosenzweig,
who took a more positive stand on Jewish law"[3] (than they do
with Martin Buber). Milton Himmelfarb echoed Potok's estimation of Rosenzweig less than one year later in his introduction to
the *Commentary* symposium on "The Condition of Jewish Belief."[4] Himmelfarb described the enormous influence of Franz Rosenzweig: "The single greatest influence on the religious thought
of North American Jewry, therefore is a German Jew – a layman
not a rabbi – who died before Hitler took power and who came
to Judaism from the very portals of the church."[5] The Rosenzweig
described by both Himmelfarb and Potok was a Rosenzweig not
yet read by the American Jewish community but one heroically
portrayed by his disciple and younger colleague, Nahum Glatzer,[6]
while the Buber described by Potok was read by the Jewish community but not yet understood because the community had not
experienced the weakening of normative structures and the anomie of unstructured existence.

The last two decades have brought many changes to the American Jewish community. The Six Day and Yom Kippur wars have

increased the sense of interdependence between American Jewry and Israel while they have also renewed the sense of Jewish vulnerability and limited freedom. The collapse of faith in the vision of America that resulted from the Vietnam experience – coupled with the marked changes in sexual practices, the decline of the family, the rise in divorce rates, prolonged single life, and the emergence of a self-conscious Jewish community – have widened the gap between the normative structures of Jewish tradition and the life practices of many Jews despite the much heralded recent return to tradition.

Perhaps the most significant change of the past two decades has been the growing awareness of the Holocaust and its shattering consequences for American Jewry. Theologically, this new consciousness has been voiced by Elie Wiesel, Richard Rubenstein, Emil Fackenheim, Eliezer Berkovits, Irving Greenberg, Arthur A. Cohen, and myself among others. This concentration on the Holocaust has also been intensified by such political developments as the rightward swing of the entire American Jewish community (with the concomitant decrease in universalism) and the general sense of Israel's increased vulnerability. Such changes have substantively altered the theological significance of Buber and Rosenzweig.

Judaism versus Christianity

In the 1970s the work of Franz Rosenzweig became accessible to the English-speaking world. Nahum Glatzer whetted America's appetite for Rosenzweig with his 1953 publication of *Franz Rosenzweig: His Life and Thought.* The publication of the correspondence between Rosenzweig and Eugen Rosenstock-Huessy in 1969 as *Judaism Despite Christianity,*[7] followed in 1971 by the translation of Rosenzweig's magnum opus, *The Star of Redemption,*[8] satisfied public interest. Both works exposed serious flaws in Rosenzweig's theology and limited his influence to doctrines on Jewish law.

Rosenzweig's correspondence with Rosenstock-Huessy had enjoyed an exalted reputation.[9] Anyone who studies the life of Rosenzweig knows the impact Rosenstock-Huessy had on him. This influence reached its climax in 1913 when Rosenzweig decided to convert to Christianity with but one reservation – he would reenact the early Christian drama by entering the church as a Jew, which resulted in his conversionary rediscovery of Judaism. This correspondence between Rosenzweig and Rosenstock-Huessy was heralded as a momentous dialogue between Judaism and Christianity, which would promote a mutual understanding of the roles both faiths were to play in the redemption of humanity. However, in reality the dialogue is not between a faithful Jew and a believing Christian but between two Jews: one who completed the final stage in the process of assimilation by converting, and the other who (when forced to the brink of conversion and faced with parental opposition)[10] renounced the assimilation and returned to Judaism.

Rosenzweig's assignment of a role for both Judaism and Christianity in redemption may be attractive to some people in this ecumenical era, yet he could not reject the Western Christian culture that had so attracted him. Rosenzweig betrays his assimilationist heritage in his uncritical adoption of Western and Christian cultural biases.

On the surface, Rosenzweig appears fully and unambivalently to accept his Judaism. He writes of the Jews:

(1) that we have the truth, (2) that we are at the goal, and (3) that any and every Jew feels in the depths of his soul that the Christian relationship to God, and so in a sense their religion, is particularly and extremely pitiful, poverty stricken, and ceremonious; namely, that as a Christian one has to learn from someone else, whomever he may be to call God "our Father." To a Jew, that God is our Father is the first and most self-evident fact – then what need is there for a third person between me and my Father in heaven?[11]

Yet Rosenzweig also maintains that the mediated relationship between the Christian and God is necessary in order for Christianity to convert the heathens and put an end to paganism. The Christian pursuit of power history and the Jewish rejection of that history are both necessary for salvation. "The synagogue bows to this anguish of denying the world for the sake of the same ultimate hope that impels the Church to bow to the anguish of affirming the world."[12]

The task of the synagogue is to fix its gaze on eternity and relinquish the domain of history to Christianity. The latter runs the risk of contamination by history in order to convert the heathens to the fatherhood of God through the sonship of Christ.

> The synagogue which is immortal but stands with broken staff and bound eyes must renounce all work in this world, and muster all her strength to preserve her life and keep herself untainted by life. And so she leaves work in the world to the church and recognizes the church as the salvation for all heathens in all time. The synagogue knows that what the works of its ritual do for Israel, the works of love do for the world outside of Israel. But the synagogue refuses to admit that the strength with which the church performs her works of love is more than "divine," that this strength is itself a power of God. Herein the synagogue gazes fixedly into the future. And the church, with unbreakable staff and eyes open to the world, this champion certain of victory, always faces the danger of having the vanquished draw up laws for her. Sent to all men, she must nevertheless not lose herself in what is common to all men. Her word is always to be "foolishness and a stumbling block."[13]

Rosenzweig's views are seriously flawed not only for their imperialistic biases and their transformation of an "is" into an "ought" (the naturalistic fallacy) but above all for the dismal and truncated existence to which Rosenzweig consigns the Jewish people. Rosenzweig recommends that the Jew accept persecution because God deems it necessary for the redemption of humanity. For Rosenzweig, exile, powerlessness, landlessness, isolation, and cultural depravity are all necessary and indeed praiseworthy because they liberate the Jew from his concerns with history and free him to serve God's eternity. (Rosenzweig used the term "an external life which is in the deepest sense unethical"[14] in reference to the sociocultural situation of the *Ostjuden* [Eastern European Jews], and in his correspondence with Rosenstock-Huessy he all too readily conceded this depravity without adding even a disparaging word about the persecution of Jews by Christians.)

Rosenzweig does not consider the Jewish situation to be the creation of human history and thus subject to change by the Jewish people; rather, he assumes some divine master plan in which the Jews are to remain as witnesses to eternity while Christianity conquers and converts the world. Rosenzweig also refuses to ask the critical question that follows his assumptions: What does history reveal of God and His ways?

Christian Mission, Jewish Victims

Rosenzweig's uncritical acceptance of the Christian mission is all the more remarkable since Jews have often been the central victims in this drama. The secularized notion of the Christian mission has served to legitimate Western imperialism, the consequences of which are clearly visible today but were also discernible as early as World War I.

Rosenzweig gives a new and somewhat pathetic meaning to the concept of the "Jewish mission to the Nations," which was so popular among German Reform Jewry during the first two decades of the twentieth century. According to Rosenzweig, powerlessness, victimization, and martyrdom are the costs the Jew must pay in order to serve as witness to eternity. Christian antisemitism is thus an expected response to the Jewish reminder that there are dimensions of existence beyond power and history.

Rosenzweig turns the traditional notion of exile on its head. According to the traditional notion of *galut,* exile was a catastrophe involving spiritual poverty and human depravity, not a celebrated opportunity to develop an internal religious life without power and self-determination. Rosenzweig's understanding of history led him to oppose the Zionist attempt to alter the Jewish condition. In fact, Rosenzweig considered Zionism a renunciation of the Jewish task within history. Rosenzweig theologically chose to legitimate – and thus perpetuate – the conditions that led to Jewish victimization, and to renounce the power that could change history. Rosenzweig applauded the truncated existence of the Jew, the depravity he was so willing to concede, as a way to remain "untainted" by the seduction of temporal history.

Upon consideration of Rosenzweig and the praise accorded his work in 1966, we must be mindful of both the changes in the Jewish community within the past twenty years and the fact that Rosenzweig was not read by many of those he influenced. Rather, his reputation was based on his stoic – and heroic – response to paralysis and his stance with respect to Jewish law. Rosenzweig's attitudes toward Jewish law can best be seeen in his dialogue with Martin Buber.

The Encounter at Sinai

Buber was aware that his own position on Jewish law was nontraditional. At points Buber even refused to discuss the law at lectures, feeling himself unable to represent the tradition and unwilling to substitute his own personal standpoint.[15] Buber's notion of the law rested on his interpretation of Israel's experience at Sinai. The Bible says: "And the Lord came down upon Mount Sinai, to the top of the mount: and the Lord called Moses to the top of the mount; and Moses went up."[16] According to tradition, the moment of revelation was not merely an encounter between Moses, Israel, and God but also a transaction in which God communicated His will to the people. According to Orthodox interpretations, the transaction involved not merely the written Torah but the Oral Law as well. To Conservative and some Reform Jews (at least as represented by the operative theological principles of their movements), the precise nature of the transaction is unclear but the fact of transaction is paramount.[17] Significant theological debates have been devoted to whether the ethical commandments alone were revealed at Sinai or both the ethical and ritual commandments, whether the whole Torah was revealed or only a part of the Torah, and whether Israel was invited to coproduce the Torah or whether God created Torah alone. Nevertheless, common to all these theological positions is the conviction that the encounter at Sinai was not formless.

The Buberian Risk

Buber strongly dissents from this transactional vision of Sinai. For Buber, this revelation was the I–You encounter par excellence in which Israel sensed God's presence and the reciprocity of relationship. The religious laws that emerged in the wake of Sinai were not God's commandments but Mosaic translations of the people's experience.[18] For Buber, God's presence was revealed at Sinai rather than an articulated law. Israel encountered God as the Eternal You, the You who could not become an "it." Israel committed itself to the spiritual struggle not to retreat from God but to stand ready for the ultimate encounter. Yet, as the biblical tale repeatedly illustrates, the people proved unequal to the task. Israel retreated into the domain of "it"; frightened by God's presence, the people turned to idolatry and created the "it" of a golden calf. The period of latency when the encounter has passed is dangerous. The human situation is lived between moments of actuality and latency. Buber writes:

> Love itself cannot abide in a direct relation; it endures, but in the alternation of actuality and latency. Every You in the world is compelled by its nature to become a thing for us or at least to enter again and again into thinghood.
>
> Only in one relationship, the all-embracing one, is even latency actuality. Only one You never ceases, in accordance with its nature to be You for us. To be sure, whoever knows God also knows God's remoteness and the agony of drought upon a frightened heart, but not the loss of presence. Only we are not always there.[19]

According to Buber, Israel and God encountered one another at Sinai. Then Israel retreated into latency and tried to give content to an experience that was inherently contentless. Israel strove to devise rules and dogmas that, according to Buber, were an attempt to make comprehensible the unconditional that the people experienced within themselves.[20] Israel gave the revelation its content as it attempted to articulate the divine presence.

Buber is not so much opposed to the attempt at objectification as he is aware of its danger. Objectification runs the risk of mediating between the person and God, of erecting a barrier that substitutes for encounter. Rules, rituals, laws, and normative structures may not only provide us with false security and with guidelines that shield us from the unpredictable; they also run the risk of becoming an "it" – an object that we possess rather then a vehicle for encounter.

> Form is a mixture of You and it too. In faith and cult it can freeze into an object; but from the gist of the relation that survives in it, it turns ever again into presence. God is near to the forms as long as man does not remove them from him. . . . Degeneration of religions means the degeneration of prayer in them: the relational power in them is buried more and more by objecthood: they find it ever more difficult to say You . . . and eventually man must leave their false security for the risk of the infinite in order to recover this ability, going from the community over which one sees only the vaulting dome of the temple and no longer the firmament into the ultimate solitude.[21]

For Buber, religious life entails risk and paradox; it is marked by essential and indissoluble antinomies, which can only be lived over again unpredictably, without the possibility of anticipation or prescription. Most of us retreat from this life of relationship. We prefer the stable, predictable, controllable world of things to the frightening and explosive dimension of relationship. For Buber, Sinai was an invitation to risk and reencounter, a call to presence and actuality.

Buber's work earned him little popularity with the representatives of normative structures or with those who had not experienced the collapse of structure during the late 1960s and early 1970s. Buber described the risk of lived actuality rather than the certitude of prescribed paths.

Rosenzweig concurs with Buber that Israel's fundamental experience at Sinai was encounter rather than transaction and that the human response took the form of law. Rosenzweig and Buber disagree over the boundary line between the human and the divine. For Rosenzweig, the boundary cannot be clearly defined. The human response, which took the form of law, can often become a vehicle for reencounter. "Law must again become commandment which seeks to be transformed into deed at the very moment it is heard. It must again regain the living reality in which all great periods have sensed the guarantee of its eternity."[22]

Personally, Rosenzweig sought to observe more and more of the *halakhah* in order to sense for himself the sacredness of its origin at Sinai. He would choose a law and continue its observance until he had personally experienced its commandedness.

In an essay entitled "Religious Authority and Mysticism,"[23] Gershom Scholem argues that tension exists between religious leaders and mystics, who are prone to trust their own experience more than external authority. However, this gap is bridged by training (the initiate generally works under the guidance of a guru or *rebbe*), by conceptual vocabulary (the mystic is usually a product of the community and hence tends to articulate his vision in traditional language even if new meaning is given to the words), and by the mystic's religious experience in which the original event that inspired the tradition is recapitulated. The path that Rosenzweig chose for himself was designed to narrow the gap between his own religious experience and the normative teachings of the *halakhic* community. He sought within his religious life to reappropriate the moment of encounter and transaction in which the people first sensed the binding quality of Jewish law.

Rosenzweig's attitude toward the law suggests a path for the rediscovery of Judaism by those returning to it from the outside. "Taste and see that the Lord is good. Happy is the man who cleaveth unto Him," says the psalmist. Rosenzweig suggests a process of spiritual experimentation, of exposing oneself to the tradition and subjectively appropriating its sacred origin. Rosenzweig and Buber agree that revelation was not a transaction, yet Rosenzweig returned to the path of law while Buber remained a religious anomist.

The dialogue between Buber and Rosenzweig did not conclude with their deaths. Today, the religious issues that divided these theologians have been revived. The resurgence of a self-conscious Jewish community, which is religious in its orientation but not fully *halakhic* in practice, has led to a renewed struggle with the normative structures of traditional Judaism. To some who come to Judaism from the secular world, and to others who were raised in traditional homes and later encountered a challenging heterodoxy, the path suggested by Rosenzweig is enormously attractive. Although I criticize Rosenzweig's thought for its endorsement of

Jewish powerlessness and Christian triumphalism, two aspects of his thought that he shares with Martin Buber are still gripping: namely, the emphasis on religious experience coupled with the rejection of law divorced from religious experience.

Whereas Rosenzweig disciplined his religious life to reengage Jewish practice, Buber transcended the particular forms of Jewish ritual in search of an experiential base for his own religious life. Rosenzweig and Buber both challenged normative Jewish structures; thus, they speak to a generation of non-Orthodox Jews who are not bound by tradition. The relational definition of the divine–human drama was compatible with the growing emphasis on human relatedness – on the relaxation of gender stereotypes in marriage, for example, in favor of the holiness of individual encounter.

Norms, Modernity, and Tradition

A modest example of the non-normative posture of many committed Jews is reflected in the *Jewish Catalog,* which has enjoyed remarkable popularity. Marshall Sklare in his controversial review of the catalogue (most appropriately published in *Commentary* – a neoconservative Jewish journal that embraces fundamentalist Christianity while remaining indifferent to Jewish religious renewal) has articulated both the attractiveness of the *Catalog* to younger Jews and his own objection to it. Sklare wrote:

> The attitude of the *Catalog*'s editors to Jewish religious law or *halachah* is the first and most obvious case in point . . . the editors exempt themselves from the central feature of Jewish religious law – its normativeness. According to Savaran and Siegel, "The *halachah* is there to inform and set guidelines, to raise questions, to offer solutions, to provide inspiration – but not dictate behavior."
>
> In most areas of life discussed within the pages of the *Catalog,* the relevant Jewish law is scrupulously reported where applicable, *but the dominant stress quickly shifts to the experiential side of the subject in question,* the side connected with issues of personal style, of taste, and aesthetic pleasure.[24]

Sklare goes on to suggest that the editors of the *Catalog* viewed *halakhah* as a life aesthetic rather than as law. Although Sklare traces the sources of this position back to their sociological origins during the late 1960s at Camp Romah in Palmer, Massachusetts (then a place of religious experimentation and spiritual ferment), and the inherent conflict in the praxis (if not the theory) of Conservative Judaism, the root of this stance is also theological. It is reflected in Buber and Rosenzweig. Mordecai Kaplan concurs that tradition should be given a voice but not a veto. The Jews addressed by the *Catalog* and the Havurah movement seek a connection with tradition but are unwilling to submit entirely to a code of behavior and belief.

The contemporary religious perspective that is most Buberian is found in the Havurah movement, yet often Havurah-oriented writers (such as Arthur Waskow) speak of creating a new *halakhah* or of removing dimensions of experience outside the domain of *halakhah*.[25] In essence, there is an unwillingness to move from the Rosenzweigian to the Buberian position, a reluctance to accept the unstructured encounter. However, the Havurah movement is basically Buberian in its emphasis on religious experience, its heterodoxy, its commitment to encounter, and its rejection of materialism in favor of the interpersonal. Nonetheless, Waskow and the movement as a whole resist the final stage of Buber's teaching, which presupposes the inadequacy of normative structures.

Buber knew that the dynamics of encounter were unstructured, unpredictable, uncontrollable, and risky. He knew that our instinct was to retreat from the fluidity of encounter into the set and comfortable world of things and structures, yet he also knew that during the most precious moments of life, structures are transcended, constraints overcome, and a radical sense of freedom combines with commitment. Buber's writings on actuality and latency indicate that life is led between the poles of structured and unstructured existence. The moments of meeting are the moments of renewal. One can rediscover the root legitimation of structures as Rosenzweig did when he discovered the commandedness of the law and the logic of formal commitment. Whoever opts for the dangerous and fragile dimension of experience, which Buber called I–You, goes beyond norms and forms.

9. The Problem of Pluralism in Contemporary Orthodoxy: Philosophy and Politics

This chapter explores why modern (liberal) Orthodoxy has had difficulty maintaining itself despite the religious resurgence of Orthodox Judaism, which is antagonistic to religious pluralism. The self-ghettoization of contemporary Orthodoxy is analyzed in this chapter from a historical, sociological, and theological perspective, especially in the work of Joseph Soloveitchik, the intellectual godfather of modern Orthodoxy, who sought a bifurcated religious consciousness where religious faith is insulated from history.

Two of Soloveitchik's disciples, David Hartman and Irving Greenberg, dissent. They offer an Orthodox approach open to historical developments such as the Holocaust and the state of Israel. Embracing pluralism, these two men have defined the parameters of contemporary Orthodox Judaism – and may well be forced to stand outside of it.

In the quarter century since I received my high school diploma from Ramaz – then considered the most liberal of all Orthodox yeshivot in America – Orthodox Judaism in America has undergone a renaissance. Although Orthodox Jews still constitute a distinct minority among American Jewry's denominations, Orthodoxy is now distinguished by a newfound sense of confidence and power. It has recovered from its precarious situation of a generation ago.

Orthodoxy now has momentum. When I was being raised, a sense of erosion plagued traditional Judaism. Seemingly, each generation of American Jewry was becoming less observant than its predecessor, less committed to tradition, less reliable in its religious beliefs. Orthodox Jews keenly felt the lure of the world beyond the community. Even for those who remained faithful, the outside world was an option – better yet, a temptation. Everyone

knew someone, usually someone quite close, who had left Orthodoxy, abandoned religious observances, and moved either into
other denominations of American Jewish life or into a strikingly
secular environment.

By contrast, in recent years the worldwide reemergence of fundamentalism, the phenomena of a *baal teshuvah* movement,[1] and
the more prevalent example of secular, Reform, and Conservative
Jews who have intensified rather than diminished their religious
observance have given Orthodox Judaism a special élan. The success of such synagogues as the Lincoln Square in New York and
suburban Orthodox prayer houses in virtually every metropolitan
area of North America – many of whose members were not raised
in Orthodox homes – have given contemporary Orthodox Jews
the sense that time is on their side.[2] They now have reason to
believe that Orthodoxy will endure and perhaps eventually triumph if not by convincing others of its veracity, then by its endurance. Orthodoxy presumes that over time, non-Orthodox
forms of Jewish life in the diaspora will wither. Traditionalists feel
that the way to get ahead is to stay the same.

Orthodox Jews seem confident that their children will remain
Jewish. Conservative, Reform, Reconstructionist, and secular
Jews appear a lot less certain that their grandchildren will be Jewish. High intermarriage rates and a wide array of other available
options require that Judaism now compete in the open market-
place of ideas and be chosen as a personal option for those American Jews who choose to remain Jews.[3] Because the outside world
no longer imposes a religious identity on the American Jew, affiliation has become a matter of choice; for significant numbers of
non-Orthodox Jews, Jewish identity is waning.

Rabbi Joseph Soloveitchik has described the double covenant of
the Jewish people as *brit goral* (the covenant of fate) and *brit yeud*
(the covenant of meaning).[4] For the first time, many American
Jews no longer feel that fate has imposed their Jewishness on
them. Jewish identity must be inner-determined because it will no
longer be externally mandated. In Sartre's terms, if it takes the
antisemite to make the Jew, with antisemitism on the decline it
may be more difficult for Jews to remain Jewish.[5] In the absence
of external coercion, Conservative and Reform Jews adopted the

same strategy that Orthodoxy used a generation ago. The Jewish day school is regarded as the first line of defense against the secular assault on Jewish identity.

Unlike other denominations, Orthodox Judaism today has a minimal gap between paid professionals and laity. By contrast, a generation ago many Jews identified with Orthodoxy although they were not Orthodox in their observance. Jews affiliated with Orthodox congregations wanted their rabbi to be Orthodox and synagogue practice to remain traditional, but they did not think that institutional affiliation must mirror private behavior. This discontinuity is currently the case within Conservative Judaism, where often the only person in the congregation whose practice reflects the movement's ideology is the rabbi. Contemporary Orthodoxy has succeeded in creating an involved, educated laity whose practice reflects the movement's basic tenets largely as a result of the yeshiva movement. In fact, some Orthodox rabbis have complained that the pressure from their congregants is for stricter observance, less compromise, and less openness to the world.

Orthodox Judaism now has a sense of its own power. In Israel, Orthodox religious parties have achieved a virtual monopoly over the religious life. Until recently, only Orthodox synagogues received state funds, and Orthodox groups received financial support disproportionate to their numbers from both the Israeli government and the Jewish Agency. Two separate government-sponsored Orthodox school systems (the second being ultra-Orthodox) are operated in Israel. From family law to Jewish dietary regulations, Orthodox Jews set the standards, administer the law, and staff the bureaucracy.[6]

The power of Israeli Orthodoxy is matched by its insulation. Structurally, Orthodox Jews live in increasingly segregated environments including separate schools, youth movements, neighborhoods, and social institutions. Even for those Orthodox Jews who serve in the army, national service is often in special units composed of like-minded adherents. Similarly, university training can be undertaken in an exclusively Orthodox environment. Separated from their fellow Jews, Orthodox leaders are under less pressure to accommodate the modern world. At home in Israel among Jews, the Orthodox are protected by nationalist sentiments from the struggle with the non-Jewish world. As a result, fanaticism and intolerance have increased, as have expressions of religious and political bigotry that in an earlier age would have been restrained.

For example, Israel's chief rabbi has forbidden Jews to sell flats to gentiles.[7] Former Sepharadi chief rabbi Ovadia Yosef ruled that if copies of the Hebrew Bible and Christian Scriptures are bound together, the latter should be ripped apart from the former and burned.[8] Similarly, Christians are increasingly referred to as *ovdei avodah zarah* (pagans) whose institutions must be destroyed according to *halakhah*.[9] There have also been savage verbal assaults on the diplomatic appointment of a Druze as Israel's consul-general in Atlanta, Georgia, because, according to Maimonides, "a non-Jew may not hold office in a Jewish state."[10]

Yehoshafat Harkabi has argued that the two clauses of *halakhah* that previously provided dispensation "for the sake of peace" and "in order not to arouse hostility" are less applicable in an Israeli context. Furthermore, invoking a dispensation avoids the core problem – the nature of these religious teachings themselves.[11]

Lest we believe that incivility is restricted to non-Jews, advertisements appeared throughout Jerusalem publicizing a rabbinic ruling that it is better for Jews to stay home on the High Holidays than to hear the shofar blown in a non-Orthodox synagogue. This intolerance may be shared by some Orthodox rabbinical authorities in the diaspora, but they are more reticent to publicize their views.

This empowerment of Orthodoxy in Israel has spread to the diaspora, where the issue is not state-endorsed power but legitimacy. Precisely because Orthodoxy is most resistant to change, it is regarded as the voice of tradition, as the authoritative interpreter of Judaism, by many Jews who are not themselves Orthodox but look for an Orthodox imprimatur to confer legitimacy. However much Conservative and Reform rabbis may complain, however often scholarly works are written that challenge Orthodox teachings, many American Jews still cite Orthodoxy even while they are unprepared to follow its teachings.

John Cuddihy has written extensively about the rule of civility in the interreligious life of America. In his work *No Offense,* Cuddihy demonstrates that pluralism and civility have led to major transformations in American religious life.[12] In the United States, Roman Catholics ceased to argue that there is no salvation outside the church. Likewise, Protestants did not proclaim that the only way to the Father is through the Son, and Jews did not speak of their chosenness outside of the prayers. In fact, the liberal pronouncements of Vatican II were first advanced by John Courtney Murray, an American Catholic theologian.

Whenever extremist religious opinions are offered in the United States, there is an immediate effort to moderate the views and hence preserve the civility of interfaith life. Consider, for example, the response to the Reverend Bailey Smith, who proclaimed that "God does not hear the prayers of the unredeemed," that is, the Jews. Smith's statement surely was not uncommon in Protestant thought, but the swift public response had little to do with the correctness of his theology. He was castigated for transgressing the unwritten law of American religious life.

American Jews have overwhelmingly embraced the religion of civility. Leonard Fein and Charles Silberman have written persuasively of the role of pluralism in the inner life of American Jews.[13] The acceptance of diverse practices and teachings, the separation of church and state, and the openness of America to multiple viewpoints all have created a climate that has allowed American Jews to flourish as never before in the diaspora. Consequently, Judaism in the United States is distinctively "American" in its passionate commitment to pluralism. Only Orthodox Jews in America dissent from this "religion of pluralism."

For the past hundred years in America and for a century and a half in Europe, Orthodox Jews were forced to accept the reality, but not the legitimacy, of non–Orthodox forms of Judaism. No one could deny the presence and power of Conservative and Reform Judaism in America, of liberal Judaism in Western Europe, and of Zionism in Israel – but there is an enormous gap between recognizing a sociopolitical religious reality and granting theological recognition.

Let us examine the case of the late revered Rav Kook the elder, the former chief rabbi of prestate Palestine. Kook was a passionate mystic and a compassionate rabbi. More than any other figure of his time, he bridged the abyss that separated the Zionist *yishuv* (pioneering settlement) from the pietistic Jewish communities living in the Holy Land. Kook is fondly remembered as a religious leader who reached out to the secular community and understood the potential of Zionism. Kook's tenure as chief rabbi is regarded as the "golden era" of mutual tolerance. [14]

Nevertheless, Kook theologically denied the legitimacy and durability of the Zionist revolution even as he described it as the dawn of redemption. Kook offered an analogy between the secular Zionist enterprise and the building of the Holy of Holies. When the holy Temple was being built, every simple worker could traverse the Temple mount and walk into the Holy of Holies. No special state of purity was required, and no special rituals observed, in order to enter the most sacred of Jewish sites, the place in the consecrated Temple that only the High Priest could enter once a year, on the Day of Atonement, after following an exacting schedule of purification. So, too, Kook told doubting pietists, secular Jews are building a Holy of Holies. Once their efforts are consecrated, only the "holy" will enter. In short, Kook viewed secular Zionism as a temporary ally in a sacred vocation. Kook never envisioned secular Zionism as a permanent reality, nor was he prepared to accept it on its own terms. Kook's views did pave the way for Orthodox Jews to cooperate with the Zionist movement.

In America, cooperation between Orthodox and non-Orthodox Jews was essential. Rabbi Joseph Soloveitchik provided such cooperative efforts with an overriding legitimacy. His distinction between "the covenant of fate" and "the covenant of meaning" provided the framework. The former is the covenant of Egypt and the latter the covenant of Sinai. Fate imposed on all Jews a shared history and often a common enemy that demanded wholehearted cooperation. Yet the covenant at Sinai divides rather than unites Jews, some of whom are prepared "to do and to hear" while others are not.

As chairman and sole member of the Orthodox Rabbinical Council of America's Halakhah Committee, Soloveitchik played a critical role in permitting intra-Jewish cooperation. Soloveitchik's precise role is currently being rewritten by some of his more strident followers, who are embarrassed by his apparent openness. (Because of poor health and advancing age, Soloveitchik withdrew from public life and teaching in 1986, and none of his would-be successors is likely to replicate – or even endorse – his previous decisions.)[15]

Soloveitchik's ruling allowed Orthodox rabbis to join the Synagogue Council of America, the national rabbinic group that includes Conservative and Reform. In the 1950s, Soloveitchik worked with Professor Saul Lieberman of the Jewish Theological Seminary toward the creation of a joint *beit din* (rabbinic tribunal) between Conservative and Orthodox rabbis to handle such issues as marriage, divorce, and conversion. The fact that such a proposal failed was due to pressures from the rabbis of both denominations; Soloveitchik voiced no theological objection.

Soloveitchik also recognized the validity of *gitten* (religious divorces) written under the supervision of Professor Boaz Cohen of the Jewish Theological Seminary. Soloveitchik's decision was binding on the Orthodox Rabbinical Council of America. In 1986, this precedent was cited by Norman Lamm, president of Yeshiva University, to indicate that the *halakhic* competence of a *beit din* – and not the institutional affiliation of its members – is critical to the acceptance of its decision.[16] Similarly, during negotiations over the Vatican II statement *Nostra Aetate* in the early 1960s, Soloveitchik and Rabbi Abraham Joshua Heschel of the Jewish Theological Seminary were in almost daily contact, acting on behalf of the Jewish people while reviewing this sensitive theological document concerning church teachings about Judaism.

The towering personality and scholarship of Soloveitchik as well as his unique record of cooperation with non-Orthodox Jews have sometimes concealed a dimension of his thought that remained impervious to religious pluralism. Until recently, the public could not easily study Soloveitchik's teaching because, by family tradition, he was reticent to publish his writings. The few works that appeared, ranging from Hebrew essays to papers in *Tradition*, were considered rare glimpses of the man's greatness. Even today, with the publication of a half-dozen works in English and a larger number in Hebrew, the power of the oral encounter between student and master cannot be re-created.[17]

In an early work, *Halakhic Man*, which is a freewheeling phenomenology of the inner life of a *mitnaged* (an opponent of Hasidism), Soloveitchik describes *halakhic* man as insulated from the world. *Halakhic* man shares elements of consciousness with cognitive man and can even operate in that universe. He also shares the sensitivities and urgency of *homo religious*, but he need not fall prey to the spiritual unrootedness nor the emotionalism and oscillation that characterize the religious life of the latter. Soloveitchik depicts the *halakhah* as a divinely revealed " a priori system" that is then applied to reality. If the Conservative movement has stressed the historicity of *halakhah* and its role as the product of the Jewish people in dialogue with revelation, Soloveitchik situates the *halakhah* outside of history as a system by which adherents orient themselves to historical events.

Like Franz Rosenzweig, Soloveitchik positions the Jewish people outside of history, engaged in applying eternal categories to transient events.

> When halakhic man approaches reality, he comes with his Torah, given to him from Sinai, in hand. He orients himself to the world by means of fixed statutes and firm principles. An entire corpus of precepts and laws guides him along the path leading to existence. Halakhic man, well furnished with rules, judgments and fundamental principles, draws near to the world with an a priori relation. His approach begins with an ideal creation and concludes with a real one.[18]

Ironically, this structural immunity to history allows Soloveitchik to consider contemporary scientific and philosophic thought without feeling threatened. Archetypal *halakhic* man is insulated but not isolated. He is blessed with an inner stability that allows him to overcome the vicissitudes of life and confront death. He can handle the turmoil of intellectual struggles in a turbulent era because his point of orientation is set, his sense of divine presence assured. "There is no real phenomenon to which *halakhic* man does not possess a fixed relationship from the outset and a clear, definitive, a priori orientation,"[19] Soloveitchik writes. In his essay "The Lonely Man of Faith," Soloveitchik distinguishes between magisterial man, the man of dignity who knows God as *Elohim,* and covenantal man, who – aware of the personal, existential, psychological drama of loneliness – encounters the personal God of revelation. Covenantal man is *halakhic* man, a Jew bound by the covenant. Soloveitchik's would-be successors are less open to the outside world, perhaps because they are less protected.

The issue of pluralism in contemporary Orthodoxy is less theological than practical, centering on four aspects of current practice: Orthodox participation in joint rabbinic bodies, marriage and divorce ceremonies, and Orthodox acceptance of individuals converted to Judaism by non-Orthodox rabbis. Although Soloveitchik approved Orthodox participation in the Synagogue Council of America, periodic attacks on that participation continue to surface. The attacks always come from the right. Orthodox rabbis threaten to withdraw whenever any change in the status quo is suggested. For example, after the Reform movement ordained women in the early 1970s, there was a move to end Orthodox participation in the New York Board of Rabbis. Ironically, the move was quashed with the very argument that delegitimated all non-Orthodox rabbis. Some Orthodox rabbis reasoned that since we "know" that Reform (or Conservative) rabbis aren't "real rabbis," what difference does it make if they are men or women? While de facto relations are always cordial and often excellent, de jure recognition presents a much greater problem.

If participation in rabbinical organizations is of little consequence to lay people, the issues of marriage, divorce, and conversion are of genuine concern, threatening a communal rift. Until divorce became widespread in the American Jewish community, the recognition of marriage presented few problems. Because *halakhah* presents three means of marriage – all of which are combined in the traditional religious wedding service with a ring, a document *(ketubah),* and a union – and because there is no inherent stigma to the unmarried, Orthodox rabbis had little reason to challenge the legitimacy of non-Orthodox ceremonies. But with the increase in divorce rates and the decision of the Reform and Reconstructionist movements not to require traditional divorces, thus raising the problem of *mamzerut* (technical bastard), the Orthodox establishment became alarmed.

According to the Torah, a child born of the union between a married woman and a man other than her husband is a *mamzer* and may not marry into the community of God for a thousand generations. Thus, a child born in a second marriage to a woman whose first marriage was not ended with a *get* (Jewish divorce papers) would be a *mamzer* since she is still technically bound to her first husband and may not again remarry. Because of the harshness of the penalty, rabbinic authorities have tended to be lenient on the question of *mamzerut*. Thus, Soloveitchik recognized on behalf of the Rabbinical Council the validity of a Conservative *get* (religious divorce), and Rabbi Norman Lamm repeated that recognition in his proposal for a joint rabbinic court. Even in Israel, where problems tend to be intensified and where there is little pressure for accommodation, Conservative divorces have been recognized without much fanfare or publicity.

In a decision that was characterized as lenient because it enabled a child who might otherwise have been considered a *mamzer* to marry, the late Rabbi Moshe Feinstein ruled that Reform marriages are not *halakhi*cally binding and hence they do not require a religious divorce.[20] Feinstein thus ruled that *mamzerut* did not apply to a child born in a second marriage when the mother's first wedding was conducted by a Reform rabbi. Since the first marriage is not deemed valid, divorce is not required and the circumstances of the child's conception is not stigmatized. Rabbi Lamm's proposal for a joint *beit din* sought to reinforce this decision by asking Reform and Reconstructionist rabbis, in the name of Jewish unity, to tell couples approaching them that the marriages they perform are not *kedat Moshe v'Yisrael* (not according to the traditions of Moses and the people Israel).[21] Thus, according to Lamm, there would be no confusion about the invalidity of the marriage by *halakhic* standards. Needless to say, Lamm's proposal – lenient, like Feinstein's *halakhic* decision – did not arouse great enthusiasm on the part of non-Orthodox rabbis.

Although the problem of pluralism primarily reflects itself in practical and seemingly insoluable problems, the issue is also theological. Only two current thinkers, Irving Greenberg and David Hartman, present a case for religious pluralism. Both are publicly identified – though not necessarily accepted – as part of Orthodox Judaism, and both seem to define its limits. The fate of either thinker may well determine the boundary of the movement.

Greenberg is most closely identified with the issue of pluralism in Jewish life. His widely publicized essay "Will There Be One Jewish People in the Year 2000?" catapulted the issue of Jewish unity to the forefront of American Jewish concerns. Although he was not the first to warn about the dangers of a schism, his essay drew significant attention, and he created the organizational apparatus to sustain and address the issue.

Greenberg offers two different arguments for religious pluralism. In his popular work, which appeared mainly in pamphlet form as organizational publications of CLAL (The Center for Leadership and Learning), Greenberg offers a spirited defense of religious pluralism. Playing the politics of the situation carefully, Greenberg walks a narrow ridge between warring camps. He builds on Soloveitchik's distinction between the two covenants. All Jews, Greenberg argues, are bound by a fourfold covenant of fate consisting of shared historical events, shared suffering, shared responsibilities (for Israel, Soviet Jewry, etc.), and shared actions (public demonstrations, acts of charity). Greenberg suggests that legitimacy is derived from and applies to all groups that share the covenant of fate. "Once having extended legitimacy, one has every right to criticize and disagree with the actions by groups that violate the covenant of destiny."[22] Thus, while Soloveitchik limited the applicability of his principle to secular Jewish and Zionist organizations but not to liberal religious groups, Greenberg extends Soloveitchik's logic to other groups. The requirement to preserve the covenant of fate, Greenberg claims, must moderate not the substance but the tone of disagreements regarding the covenant of destiny. The Jewish agenda offers a pragmatic justification for pluralism that transcends denominational differences.

Greenberg is not only a popular theologian. The accessible form of his publications often masks the intensive, consistent, systematic nature of his theological endeavor. With the exception of *The Jewish Way*, the bulk of Greenberg's works have appeared in pamphlets, oral presentations, and newspaper articles – odd but important forums for serious theological discourse.

Greenberg argues that the Holocaust and the rise of the state of Israel have initiated the third great era of Jewish history. The nature of the divine–human relationship is being transformed before our eyes. Even though the *content* of that covenant and the relationship between God and Israel have been altered, a ruptured covenant still binds Israel and God along the path to redemption. Unlike most of his Orthodox colleagues who speak of the simultaneity of the biblical and rabbinic teaching (written and oral revelation), Greenberg stresses transformations and discontinuities, the changing roles of Israel and God as well as the revolutionary impact of history.

According to Greenberg, in the biblical era God was more active with Israel. Divine intervention included commandment and historical reward. The human role was essentially passive, obedient. The symbol of the covenant, circumcision, is "sealed into Jewish physical existence, and thus is experienced in part as involuntary."[23]

In the Rabbinic era, Jews are called to a new level of covenantal existence by God. "God had constricted or imposed self-limitation to allow the Jews to take on true partnership in the covenant."[24] Direct revelation ceased, Greenberg argues, "yet even as Divine Presence becomes more hidden, it becomes more present; the widening of ritual contact with the Divine goes hand in hand with the increased hiding."[25] The Divine presence is to be found in Torah study and in deeds of kindness and graciousness; God is not only in the Temple but in a seemingly secular environment.

Greenberg also speaks of the shattering of the covenant that occurred in the Holocaust. Following Elie Wiesel and Jacob Gladstein, Greenberg recognizes that the Holocaust has altered our perceptions of God and humanity. Greenberg argues that the authority of the covenant was broken in the Holocaust, but the Jewish people – released from its obligations – chose voluntarily to renew the covenant. "We are in the age of the renewal of the covenant. God was no longer in a position to command, but the Jewish people was so in love with the dream of the redemption that it volunteered to carry our the mission."[26] Our choice to remain Jews, Greenberg argues, is our response to the covenant with God and between generations of Jews, our restatement of the response to Sinai "we will do and we will hear." The task of Jewish existence is to re-create the divine image and the human image defiled during the Holocaust, to respond to death by creating life, and to continue the journey of the Jewish people in history; in short, to bring redemption.

Beyond the pragmatic political arguments offered in defense of pluralism, essential to Greenberg's theological vision is the recognition that history has altered the form and content of Jewish life. In the generation after the Holocaust, the nature of Jewish existence must remain pluralistic. Greenberg's view of the Holocaust and his evolutionary perspective on Jewish history represent the boundary line – the limits of contemporary Orthodoxy.

While Greenberg's thinking about the covenant is influenced primarily by the Holocaust and more indirectly by the rise of Israel, David Hartman focuses on the rebirth of the Jewish state and the opportunity for a full Jewish life that the renascent state provides. Yet Hartman, too, constricts God's role in history in order to minimize God's presence at Auschwitz. Unlike his mentor and teacher Soloveitchik, Hartman is less interested in the questions of self-surrender before God. Hartman speaks of the covenant in terms that emphasize human adequacy and empowerment, the synthesis between intellect and faith.

Hartman takes pluralism for granted. Ordained by Yeshiva University, Hartman was also trained in philosophy at Fordham, a New York-based Jesuit university. Hartman's mentors thus included both Orthodox rabbis and Jesuit priests. Hartman understood and appreciated – even if he did not accept – the religious integrity of his Roman Catholic teachers. He is not reticent to quote liberal Jewish thinkers, such as Martin Buber or Abraham Joshua Heschel, whose writings he treats with respect.

The streets of New York and the environment of a pluralistic America also shaped Hartman's commitment to pluralism. He disposes of the problem quite simply:

A result of the American experience with its openness to modern philosophical currents, was to show me that people can live a significant human life without making a commitment to a personal God. What I learned in America in these various ways, can be summed up in my resolution to speak only of the value of Jewish particularity, never to make claims to know a Jewish uniqueness that demonstrates an absolute superiority of Judaism to other ways of life.[27]

Hartman makes no claim that Jews are superior or unique. He merely defends the integrity of a specific path. The Jewish way of life Hartman describes has emerged from the ghetto into American freedom; Hartman has no desire to re-ghettoize Orthodox Jews. "There are Jewish religious thinkers," Hartman writes, "who had experiences similar to mine, yet their understanding of Judaism was unaffected. They continued to perceive the system as complete; countervailing evidence was set aside. [They] did not feel called upon to reshape anything in their received tradition so as to incorporate or respond to them."[28]

Hartman also sees no need for Orthodox Jews to constrict their role in contemporary Israel, as parochial defenders of specific religious observances, without offering a vision for the totality of Israeli society. Independence, stability, and freedom allow for a more complete realization of the divine–human covenant, which can now address the entire gamut of Israeli issues from domestic welfare policy to the appropriate use of military might. Orthodoxy need not confine itself to ritualistic issues.

Hartman recognizes his subjective and selective approach to tradition. Time and again he asserts that his view is a legitimate interpretation of Jewish tradition, most specifically of rabbinic Judaism, but not the only possible reading.

Although Hartman and Greenberg differ on details and on overall conceptions, they share four fundamental convictions. The convenant is considered central to both philosophies, and in both cases history proceeds from Sinai toward redemption. For Greenberg, Judaism is currently entering its third great era, and the voluntary covenant will be reshaped to accommodate history. For Hartman as well, the covenant is voluntary, based less on coercion, as in the biblical model, than on the loving acceptance of *mitzvot* (commandments) that mediate God's presence in the world.

For both men, the image of God's relationship to the people Israel departs from a father–child model and presents a marriage motif where love, commitment, and reciprocity characterize the relationship. For both Hartman and Greenberg, the marriage motif is quite modern in its advocacy of equality, as well as intimacy and intensity, between men and women. For both men, the role of the Jewish community is decisive. Hartman writes:

> I do not wish to divide my world into two separate realms, one which is characterized by autonomous action based on human understanding of the divine norm and the other by anticipation of a dependence upon divine interventions. I prefer to see God's will for Jewish communal life, as channeled exclusively through the efforts of the Jewish community to achieve the aims of the Torah given at Sinai. . . . The sphere of unilateral divine intervention shrinks, whether in the community or in history, shrinks as the range of activities and areas of life subject to *mitzvah* increases. Jews can be encouraged and energized to act when they become conscious of the broad range of activities for which they are autonomously responsible by virtue of the Sinai covenant of *mitzvah*.[29]

Greenberg wrestles with two tendencies in American Jewish life: assimilation and the rejection of tradition on the one hand, and an Orthodoxy that seeks to divide itself from the common struggle to secure the fate of the Jewish people. He seeks to keep Orthodoxy from retreating into the ghetto and from writing off the rest of the Jewish community.

Like Greenberg, Hartman addresses two constituencies. On the one hand, Hartman seeks to demonstrate to secularist Jews the inner vitality of the living covenant that can speak to the Jewish past. He does so by describing the inner life of a *halakhic* Jew in the same categories of adequacy and self-affirmation that characterize the modern ethos. At the same time, he is fighting those aspects of Israeli Orthodoxy that reject modernity and human adequacy, relying instead on the messianic appearance of a redeemer or a saving God who can rescue Israel as it propels itself toward apocalyptic politics. While Hartman seeks to enlarge the contribution of covenantal Jews to the state and the Jewish future, he offers a more modest role for God in history and for the Jew in redemption.

A generation ago, both Hartman and Greenberg would have received a more appreciative reception from an Orthodoxy proud of the creative synthesis between modernity and tradition. Today, the very acceptance of modern categories makes Hartman and Greenberg alien to large segments of contemporary Orthodoxy. For some Orthodox Jews, the attempt at synthesis is itself alienating because even if they live in the modern world and not in a self-ghettoized environment, they prefer a bifurcated consciousness where modernity is untouched by religious consciousness and religiosity is untainted by modernity. The degree to which the thought of David Hartman and Irving Greenberg resonates within Orthodoxy reflects the community's ethos, its relationship with other Jews, and its embrace of the modern world.

10. From Auschwitz to Oslo: The Journey of Elie Wiesel

Elie Wiesel may be the single most influential Jew in America. This chapter examines Wiesel as a Jewish leader and writer. Wiesel's work resonates for those who seek to root Jewish identity in a nostalgia for the past, a mythic embrace of Soviet Jewry's heroic struggle, and the rebirth of Israel.

Wiesel personifies what Jacob Neusner has termed "the American Judaism of Holocaust and Redemption." Wiesel's role and writings reveal the attraction and limits of this Jewish ethos.

The announcement from Oslo – only hours after Yom Kippur had ended – that Elie Wiesel had been awarded the 1986 Nobel prize for peace may have come as a surprise to most Americans, but to American Jews the award seemed natural. The world had recognized what they had long known, that this child of the Holocaust, who had transformed a boy's memories of evil and destruction into eloquent testimony on behalf of the Jewish people – and all oppressed people – was the world-class spokesman for compassion, decency, and human dignity.

Wiesel has attained a unique stature within the American Jewish community. With the passing of Martin Buber and Abraham Joshua Heschel, Wiesel represents Jewish history and values to Jews and non-Jews alike. He is widely revered by all elements of the American Jewish community. He is "an icon of American Jewry's new religion of the Holocaust and Israel," remarked one nameless detractor with anger and envy as well as respect. Wiesel is also viewed by gentiles as the one non-Israeli embodiment of the Jewish people for this generation – and because he is not an Israeli, Wiesel is untainted by some of the negativity associated with Israel's policies.

Wiesel is an unusual figure among American Jewish leaders. Neither the director of an organization nor the head of a movement, he has no institutional base. Unlike Jacob Neusner or the late Gershom Scholem, Wiesel has not defined a field of scholarship. Although employed by a university (Wiesel is the Andrew Mellon University Professor of the Humanities at Boston University), he has not built a power base within academia. Widely regarded as a spokesman for Israel, he is deliberately not an Israeli and stands apart from partisan Israeli politics. In Israel, he is regarded by many as a *yored,* one who has left Israel and abandoned the quest for a national Jewish renaissance in the ancient homeland. The one institutional base he did enjoy – as chairman of the United States Holocaust Memorial Council – was rather problematic, and Wiesel was often uncomfortable with his institutional role. He resigned the eight-year chairmanship on the eve of his departure for Oslo.

Wiesel is perhaps the only Jewish leader who speaks with a charisma of person unaided by the power of office. Seemingly aloof from politics, he stands above the fray that consumes more ordinary Jewish leaders.

He is also shielded from criticism. Few organizationally affiliated Jews will take him on directly or will go on the record with their backbiting comments. His role is too significant, and he is too irreplaceable to American Jewry. Only in the Yiddish press in America and in the Hebrew press in Israel is Wiesel attacked openly – often with abandon.

Although Wiesel has influenced both Jewish and Christian theologians, he is not a religious figure in any ordinary sense. Rabbis lead their congregations; they speak from their pulpits. They are ordained by a tradition. Hasidic masters have a court and a community, disciples and students, followers and supporters. They counsel their community and have authority over their followers. Theologians propose new religious interpretations; they gain influence by virtue of their teaching. Wiesel has been called a non-Orthodox *rebbe,* the leader of a diverse group of admirers and followers, yet Wiesel does not exercise his authority in any direct way. As Robert MacAfee Brown, John Roth, and I have shown,[1] Wiesel's teachings are open to diverse interpretations depending on the background of the critic. Like a Hasidic master, Wiesel has more admirers and followers than peers or friends.

The Holocaust as Sacred Mystery

What Wiesel uniquely offers is entry into an experience, into the darkness of the Holocaust and the shadows that remain in its aftermath. The sacred mystery of our time may be the face not of God but of the anti-God, the "evil side of humanity." Through Wiesel's work and persona, the nonsurvivor is offered a glimpse at what was and is no longer, of unspeakable horror and of the painful but productive process of regeneration after destruction.

The author of more than twenty-five books, Wiesel's stature, but not his following, derives from these works. After all, most people have not read his books. (Only one, *A Beggar in Jerusalem,* has never made the best-seller list.) Of those who have read his work, fewer understand them. Followers are not sustained by the written word alone. But Wiesel's writings are significant and have stood the test of time. *Night,* his first book, is a memoir and the only book in which Wiesel deals with the Holocaust directly. Widely regarded as a classic in Holocaust literature, it is the story of a young boy – reared in the ways of Torah and fascinated by the eternity of Israel – who is rudely shocked by history as he is transported from Sighet to Auschwitz, from a world infused with God's presence to a universe apart – a world without God and man. In his early work, Wiesel struggles to find meaning for his suffering, to endow his destiny and the history of the Jewish people with a transcendent purpose. Only in his fourth book, *The Town Beyond the Wall,* does Wiesel succeed in this effort. The major character is a young Holocaust survivor who has made his way to Paris after the war. His mentor, the man who teaches him the meaning of survival, is not a Jew with memories of Sinai and Auschwitz but a Spaniard who learned of death and love during the Spanish Civil War. From Pedro, the young survivor learns two lessons that have shaped Wiesel's writings ever since. Pedro told the young man:

> You frighten me. . . . You want to eliminate suffering by pushing it to its extreme: to madness. To say "I suffer therefore I am" is to become the enemy of man. What you must say is "I suffer therefore you are." Camus wrote that to protest against a universe of unhappiness you had to create hap-

piness. That's an arrow pointing the way: it leads to another human being. And not via absurdity.[2]

Suffering can be exploited to shatter men or to heal them. It can be used to unite people or divide them. The choice is ours. The only way to redeem suffering and endow it with meaning is to treat its memory as a source of healing. In his public career and each of the twenty-two works that have followed, Wiesel has remained faithful to this insight.

Beyond Suffering

Whether writing about the struggle of Soviet Jewry or the meaning of the Bible, whether depicting pious Hasidim or alienated young Jews, Wiesel never dwells on suffering. Instead, he invokes its memory in order to teach, to rouse from indifference, to urge that more be done, to plead for Jewish pride or human solidarity, to challenge complacency.

Wiesel is a master of the spoken word. He is the premier Jewish orator of our time, a traveling *maggid* (preacher) appearing in synagogues and universities, on television and at scholarly forums, with a message that is compelling and a demeanor and voice that evokes tears and laughter, melancholy and nostalgia.

Wiesel's oral addresses, television interviews, reviews, and side comments have been collected in a three-volume work entitled *Against Silence*.[3] Like the sayings of a Hasidic master, every drop of Wiesel's teaching is now preserved for posterity.

Several themes dominate Wiesel's speeches. Wiesel is an *ohev yisrael*, a lover of Israel. He loves the Jewish people and their state, and he views Jews as central to the divine–human drama. He does not see a conflict between Judaism and universalism. The more deeply Jewish a statement or a work, the more universal its implications. Nothing provokes Wiesel's ire quite as much as a Jewish writer ashamed of his Jewishness or a gentile writer who demeans Jewish history in the name of universalism. To be a Jew is a privilege; to speak and to write of the Jews, an invitation to mystery.

Yet as chairman of the United States Holocaust Memorial Council, Wiesel was asked to find a way to speak of the special mystery of Jewish suffering during the Holocaust and the fate of other victims. For Wiesel, this problem was acute. No other writer on the Holocaust has focussed quite as much on the uniqueness of the Holocaust and on the impossibility of understanding by those who were not there. "Only those who were there will ever know," Wiesel said, "and those who were there can never tell." Ironically, because the Holocaust memorial is to be a public, government-sponsored project (even though the actual museum will be privately funded), it must include non-Jewish victims of Nazism as well as Jews. And it must tell the story to those who were not there.

The Poet as Political Leader

As chairman of the Council, Wiesel walked a tightrope between parochialism and universalism that often threatened to break. "While not all the victims were Jews," Wiesel wrote to President Carter, "all Jews were victims"[4] subject to a fate that set them apart from other people. Those who know Wiesel well, or who have worked with him on the project, realized that he was torn. For more than a quarter of a century, Wiesel has almost single-handedly shaped the story of the Holocaust that American Jews tell their children. He emphasizes the magnificence of the world that preceded the destruction, the total evil – unprecedented in scope, intention, and execution – and the sacred miracle of rebirth. There is little place in Wiesel's work for the non-Jew in a role other than bystander or perpetrator.

Wiesel's Holocaust tale enhances Jewish uniqueness. Jews remain the chosen people, chosen by God at Sinai and selected by the anti-God at Auschwitz. Jews are a people set apart. Defying understanding, their history can not be captured in conventional categories.

Unlike other American Jewish authors, Wiesel has seldom written of himself as an American. He came to the United States when he was almost thirty; he was well aware of the American failure to rescue homeless Jews or to bomb the camps during the Holocaust. Thus, America never had the allure for Wiesel that it had to a generation of immigrant Jewish authors such as Henry Roth, Bernard Malamud, Saul Bellow, Philip Roth, or Chaim Potok. Yet as chairman of the U.S. Holocaust Memorial Council, Wiesel was asked to shape a story of the Holocaust that speaks to American values and resonates with the national experience. After almost nine years and the Nobel prize, it was a responsibility Wiesel no longer welcomed. He feared dejudaization of the Holocaust, but he knew that a memorial that considered only the Jewish experience would not find its appropriate place on the national mall.

Dreams and Reality

A novelist is omnipotent, controlling all aspects of the reality he shapes. A political leader – and every presidential appointee is a political leader – must deal with the pulls of diverse and often conflicting constituencies. Ironically, the man who shaped the Jewish story, who had assiduously avoided grappling with the American story, was called upon to shape the American tale of the Holocaust.

Wiesel once wrote that he envies Soviet Jews because only in the Soviet Union is Israel still a dream, if not a prayer. When Wiesel speaks of Soviet Jewry, he does not deal with *olim* and *noshrim* (those Soviet Jews who go to Israel and those who are pejoratively considered "dropouts" because they choose to make their home in the West and not in Israel), or the politics and personalities of the movement. Removed from politics and hard policy decisions, Wiesel's concern is with the mystery of Jewish survival and the tenacity of Jewish yearning. Six decades after the revolution, the desire of Russian Jews to be Jewish is not extinguished. Wiesel tells and retells tales of their joy, not their suffering – of massive gatherings on Simchat Torah (the jubilant festival celebrating a complete reading of the Pentateuch), of greeting Golda Meir (Israel's first ambassador to the Soviet Union) in 1948. Wiesel elevates the struggle and the drama, recapturing the sacred and avoiding the mundane. He tries to shape a story that, even if detached from political realities, can faithfully capture an inner truth.

Twenty years to the day after his last Simchat Torah visit, Wiesel was greeted as a Nobel laureate by thousands of Soviet Jews celebrating ancient endings and new beginnings, cheering his award and overcoming the fear and intimidation to enjoy a Jewish celebration. With the improvement of Soviet-Jewish relations brought about by Gorbachev's policies of *glasnost,* Wiesel was invited by Soviet Jews to open their first Jewish Community Center in 1989.

Wiesel writes of Israel with love and respect, above all with gratitude. He is a defender of Israel against all accusers. He recognizes the nobility of Israel, the contributions of Israel, and the unique responsibility of Israel to be a state and more than a state – a home even to the dispersed and a symbol of pride for Jews everywhere. Wiesel also speaks of Israel as a dream unsullied by its less than dreamlike reality. In his writings and speeches, the miracle of 1967 is recounted. The urgency of 1973 and the drama of Sadat's visit to Jerusalem are all recaptured.

Wiesel will not criticize Israel outside Israel except on rare occasions – and thus in his entire corpus there are striking omissions; he has uttered barely a word on Lebanon or on the territories, nothing on the economy or Kahane. He has made no mention of religious fanaticism and the politics of messianism, and he offers no perspective on the relationship between Israel and the diaspora or on the *intifada.*[5] Instead, Wiesel spins tales that are rich, poignant, and moving.

Time and again, Wiesel is asked by Israelis: "Why are you not here?" Wiesel responds that he is unworthy. Because he treats Israel as a dream and has chosen not to live there, his words resonate most among diaspora Jews. The same story that might arouse passion and love within the diaspora is a cause of fury in Israel.

Of course, Wiesel speaks of the Holocaust – often indirectly. It lurks in the shadows, but it is for him the central mystery of the contemporary world, a harbinger of truths unfathomable, an event so disturbing that some choose to avoid it and others to dilute it. Despite a schedule that includes scores of lectures throughout the United States, Canada, and France, Wiesel protests that he prefers silence. Seemingly, he protests too much. After all, how can one speak time and again and then ask for silence? How can one write book after book and then insist that words are unequal to the task?

Martin Buber once wrote of the I–You experience:

> The more powerful the response, the more powerfully it ties down the You and as by a spell binds it into an object. Only silence toward the You, the silence of all tongues, the taciturn waiting in the unformed, undifferentiated, prelinguistic word leaves the You free and stands together with it in reserve where the spirit does not manifest itself but is. *All response binds man into the It-world. That is the melancholy of man, and that is his greatness.*[6]

Even as Wiesel speaks and writes, he knows that he runs the risk of turning the sacred mystery of the Holocaust into an "it." Silence is a temptation but not a serious alternative.

Wiesel speaks of God with anguish. He wrestles with God and against God, he tells of the trial of God, but he never abandons God or renounces the tradition. He remains private with regard to his own religious life, concealing far more than he reveals. One will often read stories of deep personal and private piety, of Wiesel's return to Orthodox praxis. Like the stories of the life of a Hasidic master, mystery obscures the truth but enriches the drama.

Shadows of the Holocaust

Wiesel speaks of the world that preceded the Holocaust with tenderness and love, unwilling to disturb a child's picture of a sanctified, majestic world. Sabbath is the *Shabbos* of Sighet, not the seventh day observed in New York or even Jerusalem. Religious life before the war had integrity, passion, and depth. Jewish life today is but a pale reflection of that world.

Wiesel always speaks as a Jew, but he never speaks only of Jews. His voice is raised on behalf of all who are in pain, all who are in need of refuge. He was among the first to act on behalf of the Cambodian and Vietnamese boat people. He works on behalf of black South Africans and starving Ethiopians as he once had for Biafrans. He has asked for refuge for Central Americans and for Iranian Bahais as he has pleaded for Soviet Jews. Wiesel considers all these events a shadow of the Holocaust, a reflection of an evil unleashed within the planet whose mysterious implications are not yet known.

Only one event is deemed worthy of the name Holocaust – a burnt offering whole before the Lord – and that is the nuclear holocaust that may come unless. . . . The sentence is never completed because Wiesel does not offer a pragmatic program. He doesn't deal with throw weights or with Star Wars, with the balance of power or Mutually Assured Destruction. Instead, he speaks with the passion of a poet and the dire warnings of a prophet.

For some, a Nobel prize might be the end, the crowning glory of a life well lived. For Elie Wiesel, the prize may be a new beginning. At sixty, he is still a relatively young man. The symbol of American Jewry's encounter with the Holocaust, he has tried to focus on the past in the interest of the future.

11. Jacob Neusner and the Renewal of an Ever-Dying People

No one has offered a more poignant and serious critique of the Holocaust's role in American Jewish life than Jacob Neusner. This chapter profiles Neusner as a scholar and highlights his demurral from American Jewry's attempt to build its future on the ashes of Auschwitz. In the end, Neusner finds no way to circumvent the Holocaust.

Jacob Neusner is a phenomenon in contemporary scholarship. At fifty-eight, he is the author of more than 170 books and the editor of scores more. His students hold some of the most prestigious appointments in universities throughout the world. Neusner is in the midst of at least five multiyear, multivolume projects. Under his leadership, all the major texts of classical Judaism will be translated into English in an avalanche of work that would take lesser scholars a lifetime. Neusner is still growing intellectually, still refining his thoughts.

No contemporary scholar in the humanities is as dominant in his field as Neusner. His influence can be felt in the study of religion, both ancient and modern. His specialties are the Talmud and the interaction between Judaism and Christianity. As a scholar, Neusner is not only prolific but wide-ranging. He has written works as diverse as a history of the Jews of Iran (Persia) and the first English translation of the long-neglected Talmud of the Land of Israel (*Talmud Yerushalmi*). He has written biographies of rabbinic masters and rewritten them as his thinking changed.

Neusner came to the study of Talmud rather late in life. Raised as a Reform Jew in suburban West Hartford, Connecticut, he concentrated on classical rabbinic texts only after he completed his undergraduate education at Harvard and a postgraduate year at Oxford. Thus, he began his studies at an age by which most would-be rabbinic scholars had already spent ten or more years studying the Talmud as part of their elementary, high school, and yeshiva education. Because Neusner lacked early training, he was unburdened by tradition and convention. Unlike three generations of Jewish scholars who began their rabbinic studies at yeshivot and only later moved into the strange, exciting, pluralistic, and secular world of the university, Neusner was well grounded in secular learning before he began his Talmudic study. His late entry into the world of rabbinic learning also meant that he did not become a disciple of the Jewish Theological Seminary's professor of Talmud, Saul Lieberman. Neusner was too young, too inexperienced, to be trained by the master.

Neusner's early training as a journalist – his father was the editor and publisher of the *Connecticut Jewish Ledger* – taught him to write quickly and on a deadline and kept him far removed from the ponderous ethos of rabbinic scholarship where years are spent crafting an article and a lifetime writing a long book.

During the past half decade, Neusner has studied the classics of ancient Judaism as single works, systematically excluding all other texts – contemporaneous or later commentaries – in order to discover the individuality of a specific work. He thus wrote on the Mishnah in *Judaism: The Evidence of the Mishnah;* on the Palestinian Talmud in *Judaism in Society: The Evidence of the Yerushalmi;* on the more widely known Babylonian Talmud in *Judaism: The Classical Statement, The Evidence of the Bavli;* as well as on specific works of the Midrash, such as Leviticus Rabbah. These projects now completed, Neusner is currently probing Judaism as a system. Recent books deal with the emotional, ritual, and theological components of classical Judaism.

Even Neusner's sojourns – pauses between sustained projects – are intriguing. He finds that less ambitious projects are the best way to release restless energy. Thus, Neusner has written books on specific topics within rabbinic literature, such as the role of story, the concept of the Messiah, Judaism without Christianity, and Jewish Christianity. He has written texts for adults and children, including *An Invitation to the Talmud* and *Pirkei Avot,* a work on *tzedakah* (philanthropy), and a reader on the Palestinian Talmud. He is widely known by college students for candid comments in his book *How to Grade Your Professors and Other Unex-*

pected Advice, which (despite the apparent frivolity of its title) is a sharp and serious critique of higher education.

Periodically, Neusner abandons the ancient world to write about issues in contemporary Judaism. At first, these forays into the modern world were confined to texts for classes or to introductory works on Judaism. As a university professor and Ungerleider Distinguished Scholar at Brown University, Neusner adopted a tradition common in the scientific disciplines but all too rare in humanistic studies. A senior scholar, he taught introductory undergraduate courses. The results were a boon to Judaic studies because they resulted in textbooks of extraordinary quality and authority.

Later, Neusner published collections of his essays, organized thematically around current issues. Thus, in *Stranger at Home* Neusner focuses on the role of the Holocaust and the State of Israel in Jewish life. He challenges those who have overemphasized the Holocaust and explores the problems that Zionism poses for Judaism as well as, in turn, the problems that Judaism poses for Zionism.

Neusner's focus on the Holocaust is in continuity with his work in classical Judaism because he formerly studied how the rabbis reunited the Jewish people after the destruction. Neusner examined how these religious leaders set the agenda for the tenth of Av in the year 70 C.E., the morning after the Temple was left in ashes. The urgency of this question parallels the experience of a young boy who reached the age of bar mitzvah in the weeks immediately after World War II.

Singularly unorthodox, Neusner's work – historical or contemporary – provokes fellow scholars and rabbis as well as Jewish community leaders. He escapes all conventional definitions and resists categorization. On the one hand, Neusner is the most prolific and persuasive advocate of the secular study of Judaism – ancient and modern. Yet he is also deeply committed to the religious enterprise of the people, Israel. In *Israel in America: A Too Comfortable Exile?* Neusner writes of leading a holy life as a Jew in America. He does not often address Zionist politics or geopolitical issues facing the modern state but writes about the role of the secular Israeli state in the holy vocation of the people Israel. To the religious, Neusner appears secular. To the secular, he seems profoundly religious. To the Zionists, he is an ardent defender of Jewish life in America, and to assimilated American Jews he is an unapologetic champion of Jewish life.

Neusner raises issues that others would prefer to avoid, such as the residue of fundamentalism that underlies much of contemporary Jewish scholarship. Neusner's work is often controversial, particularly because it cuts against the grain of contemporary thinking. In April 1987, Neusner set off quite a debate by asking the question that challenged the core of contemporary Zionist pretensions: "Is America the Promised Land?" To American Jews, the answer was obvious but remained unspoken. Jews have never enjoyed a country quite as much nor prospered socially, materially, and intellectually as they have in the United States. To Israelis, who come to the United States by the tens of thousands, and to Soviet Jews, who, when offered the choice, chose to migrate to the United States rather than Israel in ratios of more than eight to one, the answer to Neusner's question may be equally obvious – but it remains shrouded in mystery. Israel is the homeland of the Jews, but in record numbers Jews from around the world are choosing to make their home in the United States rather than Israel. Typically, Neusner raised the issue and refused to shrink from the consequences – ideological, religious, and historical. In *The Jewish War Against the Jews,* Neusner probes the divisions that are ripping Jews apart. Despite the veneer of apparent unity, wars are raging – and they are ugly.

Neusner's work is often controversial, particularly because it is direct and runs against the conventions of Jewish thinking. When Neusner enters a disagreement, he usually conducts it in the public domain; in books, newspaper articles, and open letters.

Of all contemporary Judaic scholars, Neusner is the most American. Fully integrated into the university community, he pragmatically probes problems, asking questions and seeking evidence that can yield an answer. Neusner violates a norm of rabbinic scholarship by refusing to wait until he knows everything to write something. When Neusner makes mistakes, he admits them. When he discovers something that contradicts or sharpens his earlier thinking, he writes another book.

In *Death and Birth of Judaism,* Neusner asks the following question: What happens when Judaism of the Dual Torah (his term for classical Judaism) no longer appears self-evident to its followers? In his analysis, Neusner posits six Judaisms (the plural is deliberate) of modern times – Judaic systems that emerged in the aftermath of emancipation in postrevolutionary America and France: Reform, Orthodox, and Positive Historical (Conservative) Judaism; Zionism and Jewish socialism/Yiddishism; and the American Judaism of Holocaust and redemption (which has emerged in the last two decades).

In his earlier work on classical Judaism, Neusner held that Judaism of the Dual Torah emerged as a self-conscious response to Christianity. The idea of two revelations at Sinai – oral and written – was not present in the Mishnah (edited c. 200 C.E.); it emerged only in the Talmud Yerushalmi, in the aftermath of Rome's first Christian emperor, Constantine. The evolving concept of Judaism answered three questions that sprang from the expanding Christian milieu: What was Israel (the Jewish people)? What was expected of Israel? And what is the meaning of history?

"The Judaism of the canon," Neusner writes, "flourished when the world to which it spoke found persuasive not the answers alone but the very questions deemed paramount and pressing. And that Judaism ceased to speak to Jews when its message proved incongruent to questions Jews found they had to answer."[1]

In the modern world, Jews face questions posed not by Christianity but by a secular state. The meaning of Israel – the people, not the state – therefore took on a new definition.

Characteristically, the first Jewish answer was theological. Reform Judaism set the theological agenda by the questions it asked regarding the continuity between Israel of the past and Israel of the future. Although the answers that Reform Judaism gave were rejected by other denominations, the questions it asked – and the evidence cited – were common to all three movements. Jewish continuity was to be found in the past: in rereading the past.

For Neusner, the differences between Reform, Orthodox, and Conservative Judaism are a matter of degrees, stages along a continuum, which are exaggerated by what C. Wright Mills has called "the tyranny of petty differences."

For Reform Judaism, the modern ethos was determinative. For the Conservative movement (the Positive Historical school), history established what part of the past was authoritative. Orthodox Judaism lived seemingly untouched by history in a split consciousness: in the world, but apart from the world. Its view of the people Israel changed Orthodoxy as a movement. Common to all three Judaisms was the quest for continuity with the past and the need to confront altered circumstances.

The final two Judaisms of the nineteenth century were revolutionary, not evolutionary, Judaisms. They did not seek legitimacy from the immediate past en route to the future. The Zionists negated European Jewish existence – indeed, the entire diaspora. They "reinvented the past," rereading history in quest of heoric forebearers and abruptly skipping over those periods of exile that could not nurture an independent Jewish state. Masada, the site of nationalistic suicide, became a symbol – not Yavneh, where scholarship replaced priestly worship after the second Temple's destruction. Bar-Kokhba, the leader of the failed uprising in 132–35 C.E., became a hero – not Yochanan ben Zakkai, who fashioned a landless, Templeless Judaism after 70 C.E. (a religious approach that lasted for almost two millennia).

As a system, Zionism answered fundamental questions: "Who is Israel?" The Zionist answer specified that the Jewish people were to become a nation like any other. What should Israel do? Zionism responded that the people must labor to create an independent state. What is the eschaton? The establishment of that state.

Neusner shared David Ben-Gurion's belief that Zionism died as a form of Judaism precisely at the moment it succeeded and was superseded by Israeli nationalism. Why did Zionism succeed? In part because history raised the overriding question to which Zionism responded: the political condition of the Jews after World War II. Zionism had a compelling answer to the questions Jews were forced to ask: sovereignty and an army.

The final Judaic system of the nineteenth century, Jewish socialism and Yiddishism, perished in the Holocaust. For socialists, the fundamental definition of Israel was economic. They required worker solidarity and *Menschlichkeit* (humaneness). Socialism and Yiddishism anticipated a revolution, but before it came Jews were swept into the gas chambers. Afterward, Jews had difficulty believeing in man or God, and the Yiddish-speaking world of Eastern Europe was no longer.

American Judaism after the Six Day War has been characterized by Neusner as the Judaism of Holocaust and redemption; the stories Jews tell about their Jewishness have less to do with their own circumstances than with what happened to another Jewish community four decades ago, and what Americans have chosen not to become – Israelis. Who is Israel (i.e., the Jewish people) according to this view? Those who could have been victims of the Holocaust (all Jews) and those who are willing to work against its recurrence. What does Israel do? Philanthropy, politics, and organizational life.

Although Neusner has been a vital contributor to this American Jewish renaissance, which he celebrates, he is not optimistic about the longevity of this system. He cites four reasons.

"The Judaic system of Holocaust and Redemption leaves unaffected the larger dimensions of human existence of Jewish Americans – and that is part of that system's power."[2] However, as people look for answers to the other dimensions of their lives, the vicariousness of American Jewry's new theology does not serve them well.

Second, Neusner bemoans an intellectual demise. American Judaism of Holocaust and redemption works only with what is near at hand, "the raw materials made available by contemporary experience – emotions on the one side, and politics on the other. Access to realms beyond require learning in literature, the only resource beyond the immediate."[3]

American Jews, unlike their ancestors, no longer regard being Jewish as a matter of intellect. Unlike all other Judaisms of the nineteenth and twentieth centuries, the Judaism of Holocaust and redemption is the product not of intellectuals but of bureaucrats, fund-raisers, administrators, and public relations people. In Neusner's eyes, this Judaism lacks spirit and charismatic leadership.

"The correlation between mass murder and a culture of organizations proves exact: the war against the Jews called forth from the Jews people capable of building institutions to protect the collectivity of Israel, so far as anyone could be saved. Consequently, much was saved. But much was lost."[4]

In the end, the consummate historian-empiricist becomes a theologian:

> The first century found its enduring memory in one man on a hill, on a cross; the twentieth, in six million men, women, and children making up a Golgotha, a hill of skulls of their own. No wonder that the Judaism of the age struggled heroically to frame a Judaic system appropriate to the issue of the age. No wonder they failed. Who would want to succeed in framing a world view congruent to such an age, a way of life to be lived in an age of death.[5]

Neusner sees some hope in the current return to Judaism. Jews are looking for a way back, a way to experience themselves as Jews – to live a holy life and find a meaningful future. Historians describe dilemmas. Theologians must chart paths. The problem remains: How does one live in continuity with the past after Auschwitz and Israel, when Jewish life has been so discontinuous?

12.   Political Zionism's Would-Be Successors: Sectarianism, Messianism, Nationalism, and Secularism

For the past two decades, Zionism has been the dominant ideology of world Jewry. Although Zionism has succeeded brilliantly, it has failed to realize four of its initial goals. Forty years after achieving statehood, Jews remain a vulnerable, abnormal, and interdependent people living in the diaspora as well as in their homeland.

Those Jews who live in Israel can agree neither on the core achievement of the Zionist movement nor on the direction it must chart in the future. Israel is unable to resolve the tension between a democratic Jewish state and the incorporation of Arab-inhabited lands in biblical Israel. This problem, exacerbated by religious zealotry endemic to the region, has given rise to apocalyptic politics among an influential, messianically oriented minority of Israelis.

The outcome of this tension may well shape the boundaries of Israel and its relationship with both American Jewry and the Western world.

This chapter offers an analysis of Zionism's failure to realize its dreams, and of the turmoil that has been created by conflicting ideologies struggling for preeminence after Labor Zionism collapsed as Israel's civic religion.

In no region of the world is the relationship between religion and politics more pronounced and probed than in the Middle East. The rise of militant Islam, the fanaticism – and willingness to accept martyrdom – of Ayatollah Khomeini and his followers, the rivalry between Shi'ite and Sunni Moslems, the struggle between Moslems and Christians in Lebanon, the Arab-Jewish wars of the past sixty years, and the tensions between observant and secular Jews in Israel, have all focused attention on the problem. Yet most treatments of the social and political developments in contemporary Israel have been shallow at best in their consideration of the complex interaction of religion and politics endemic to the region. When social analysts have considered the problem of religion and politics in Israel, they have generally analyzed state-supported religion and its clerical functions or the process by which traditional Judaism – itself the product of diaspora and powerlessness – has been transformed by the modern state.

Even the most sensitive observers have often limited themselves to the dynamic of religious parties and the compromises with tradition compelled by statehood.[1] Such issues are certainly interesting and important; it is compelling, for example, to investigate changes in a religious framework (formed when Jews had neither the possibility nor obligations of power) required to accommodate the Jewish people in a Jewish state responsible for all services – the army, industry, police, transportation, judiciary, and so on. However, the most critical religious developments in contemporary Israel – namely, the shift from clerical demands for religious observance to ideological predominance in the state – has gone largely uninterpreted.[2] Religious parties have intensified their agenda, not only pushing Orthodox demands for religious conformity by other segments of Israeli society but also trying to impose their territorial views.

Ironically, while social living patterns, educational structures, and even army services for religious Jews have become more ghettoized, religious politics have moved ideologically out of the ghetto. The rise of the Likud Party, the growth of nationalism, the militancy of religious messianism (Gush Emunim), and the weakening of Israel's Labor Party spring from demographic, political, social, and economic realities, but purely religious factors are also involved.[3] Underlying religious values affect the power complex and the national goals that shape the political horizon.

The Lure and Failure of Emancipation

Classical Zionism originated in reaction to harsh events. Political Zionism actually had two births: the first in 1881 with Leo Pinsker's book *Auto-Emancipation* (yet at that time the movement was stillborn), and the second in 1897 with Theodore Herzl's political program and the Zionist movement he shaped. Pinsker's book was little known but most powerful. In fact, years later when Herzl finally read Pinsker's work, he indicated that had he known of its existence, he would never have written *The Jewish State*. Pinsker's writings reflected his disappointment with the process of emancipation; by the time of the 1881 pogroms, Jews in czarist Russia faced death, conversion, or emigration. In response to this violence, two processes began that were to reshape contemporary Jewish history: massive immigration to the United States, and a more limited immigration to Palestine.

Herzl's writings were also the product of his disappointment with history.[4] The Dreyfus trial convinced Herzl that emancipation could not solve the Jewish problem. European antisemitism was too pervasive. As exceptional Jews, Pinsker and Herzl were both pariahs, standing outside their own community yet at the same time alienated from gentile society. History had revealed to them the impossibility of their situation and the futility of a purely personal solution to the "Jewish problem." Both men proposed a political alternative that was to form the core of Zionist ideology.

The Zionist vision was fourfold. It sought to normalize the Jewish people, achieve political independence, end Jewish vulnerability, and gather exiled Jews scattered throughout the diaspora. Whereas for other Zionist thinkers this vision was merely a prelude to spiritual or religious revolution (Ahad Haam or Rav Kook), for Pinsker and Herzl – and for Baruch Spinoza centuries earlier – the political solution was an end in itself.

The Politics of Normalization

Normalization has been a goal for many Jews since the beginning of emancipation in 1789. Originally, it found expression in the desire for citizenship and the abolition of discrimination. The quest for normalization began as a movement of elite Jews whose contacts with the gentile world were increasing. This agenda was soon given an intellectual infrastructure to legitimate its claims. The movement of *Wissenschaft des Judentums* (the Science of Judaism) was another manifestation of the desire for normalcy. The Wissenschaft movement attempted to understand Jewish existence without resorting to the supernatural or the extraordinary. The conventional categories of social, scientific, humanistic, and historical inquiry were applied to the study of Judaism. Jewish religious leaders – conservative by nature and design – were suspicious of the Wissenschaft movement. They regarded normalization as a renunciation of the unique role of the Jewish people. Even those religious thinkers who sought to limit the social stigma of Jewish differences were reluctant to abandon an explicitly supernatural vocation for the Jewish people. Only Mordecai Kaplan in early twentieth-century America was willing to relinquish the concept of chosenness and see Jewish life within its natural dimensions.[5]

However much Jews sought normalcy, their status in Europe – described by Hannah Arendt and others as "between pariah and parvenu" – denied them the possibility of the normal situation they ardently desired. Unique to Zionism was the possibility of achieving normalization not for an individual Jew but for the Jewish people as a whole.

Herzl's dream was that Jews would form a state like any other state, the Switzerland of the Middle East – clean, efficient, well-organized, without significant controversy (in short, boring). For some early Zionists, normalcy required the inversion of Jewish economic status, a return of Jews to the working class as farmers and factory laborers, as shepherds and bus drivers, along with the more traditional roles (in Western European countries) of middlemen, teachers, scholars, bankers, and small entrepreneurs. The early newspapers of Tel Aviv even celebrated the return of the Jewish people to normalcy by taking particular pride in the arrest of the first Jewish criminals and prostitutes in the early prestate period. Herzl and the political Zionists felt that normalization could be achieved only by the resumption of Jewish political life and the eventual acquisition of sovereignty and power – a state and an army.

Initially, the Zionist platform was a minority position among the Jewish people, denied by many segments of Orthodoxy (which rightly regarded Zionism as an agent of secularization), by Reform Jewry (which was uncomfortable with any assertion of Jewish nationalism and peoplehood), and by those seeking a personal solution to the Jewish problem in either Europe or America (for whom the plan was considered unnecessary). Only the most extreme manifestation of Jewish abnormality as expressed in the Holocaust later convinced the vast majority that not only was normalcy desirable but Zionism was the only way to achieve it.

Jacob Neusner has brilliantly described the aftermath of the second Temple's destruction in 70 C.E. when Jews lost their political independence and the capacity for self-defense yet retained spiritual independence and self-government.[6] Under these conditions, Jewish life was dependent on the consent of the sovereign and the goodwill of others who maintained a near monopoly on the instruments of power. As we have seen, the great German Jewish theologian of the early twentieth century, Franz Rosenzweig, turned this regrettable reality into a celebrative theology. For Rosenzweig, the task of the Jew was to gaze at eternity untouched by the vicissitudes of history and uncorrupted by the exercise of power.[7] For Rosenzweig, Judaism was the goal and Christianity the way. Christianity's task was to convert the world to the belief in one God through its coercive political power. Compromise and corruption were thus permitted. Although Rosenzweig enjoyed a distinguished following in prewar Germany and postwar America, his teachings have been overwhelmingly rejected by the Jewish people, who, in the aftermath of the Holocaust, moved toward political independence and chose to enter power history.

After World War I, Jewish leaders in Europe and America argued for the protection of Jewish rights as part of a guarantee for minority rights in majority cultures. Not so after the Holocaust. From the Biltmore Conference of 1943 onward, Jews enthusiastically supported the call for Jewish independence. They wanted to end their reliance on the benevolence of humankind and the compassion of world leaders.

The Decision to Enter History

Herzl considered Jewish independence a matter of will. David Ben-Gurion would say in moments of despair: "I don't care what the nations [goyim] think; what concerns me is how the Jews act." Echoes of this position resounded in Menachem Begin's defiance of America and his oft-proclaimed and exaggerated annoyance at Israel's presumed status as a "banana republic." Sovereignty and power were not only needed to achieve normalcy for the Jewish people; they were also expected to end its dependence on the nations of the world and permit it the freedom of nonapologetic self-expression.

Similarly, the quest for power was motivated by a desire to end vulnerability. A sovereign Jewish state could guarantee its own security and transform the image of the Jew both at home and abroad. Israel was to stand as the guarantor of Jewish safety throughout the world. Jews could now assume a new posture as fighters and farmers – assertive rather than submissive – unbowed by the weight of centuries of oppression and impotence.[8] If normalization was the strategy to end antisemitism (a tactic suggested by both Freud and Herzl), then independence was a prerequisite for developing sufficient power to end Jewish vulnerability. The stories that Israelis often tell at state occasions celebrating their independence or memorializing the Holocaust are instructive, for they represent not only a break with tradition but a reassertion of human initiative in Jewish history.

A New Self-Consciousness

In the traditional rendition of the Passover story, God is regarded as the central actor within Jewish history. The name of Moses does not even appear in the Passover story, for "God – not an angel nor a messenger" – is depicted as the agent of redemption. In the traditional observance of Hanukah and Purim, the two holidays that celebrate Jewish political and diplomatic victories over oppression, God is given major credit for victory. By contrast, former prime minister Yitzhak Rabin recalled at his final Holocaust commemoration while in office (May 1977) that Jewish resistance in the Warsaw Ghetto was essentially unarmed. Jewish fighters were forced to match their naked strength against the power of the Nazi army. Armed more by courage than weapons, Rabin said, they resisted until their deaths. Rabin declared: "Now that we have a Jewish state, Jewish fighters need not proceed unarmed. They can now defend themselves and protect their families – their wives, their mothers, and their children." The traditional *Haggadah* reads: "In every generation they rise against us to destroy us, but the Holy One, Blessed Be He, saves us from their hands." In contrast, Israelis now proclaim that the Jewish people themselves shall have the means of self-defense against those who would seek to destroy them. This transformation in consciousness was reflected in bumper stickers that appeared just after the 1967 Six Day War. "Israel, trust in TZHAL" (The Israel Defense Forces). This motto substitutes the word "army" in the place of divinity; the psalmist said: "Israel, trust in the Lord."

According to the classical Zionist vision, the emergence of the state was to end Jewish vulnerability not only within Israel but throughout the diaspora because those who would oppress Jews would soon learn that Jewish blood could not be shed without consequence. Undoubtedly, the founding of Israel and its successful defense against destruction in 1948, 1967, and 1973 added immeasurably to Jewish pride and to the hold of the state on the Jewish people. In addition, for nearly three decades there was a direct correlation between the growth of the state as a viable national entity and the decline of antisemitism.[9]

Ingathering of the Exiles

The fourth of the Zionist dreams was the ingathering of the exiles. Jews were expected to migrate from the four corners of the earth to return to their ancestral homeland, while the remaining diaspora, faced with assimilation and persecution, would wither away. Diaspora communities would progressively weaken both culturally and religiously as productive centers of Jewish life. Israel was to become the heart of Jewry, contributing to the welfare of the diaspora and eventually witnessing its extinction. The creativity of an assertive, nonapologetic Jewish culture – speaking its historic language – was to eclipse the creativity of diaspora communities by the quality of its creations, their authenticity and cultural integrity. This fourfold vision dominated the prestate years of the Zionist movement and the initial decades following the establishment of the state.

Ironically, although Zionism succeeded beyond its wildest imagination, its ideological underpinnings have been severely challenged by recent events. On the one hand, no one at the time of Herzl could have imagined that within half a century a Jewish state would become a reality, that it would possess the ability to defend itself, that it would absorb more than 2 million Jews, that it would become a regional power, and that it would develop an advanced technology capable of making deserts bloom. On the other hand, many of the events of the past decade have shown the inadequacies of the fourfold vision, the failure of which has generated religious and nationalistic myths in an effort to fill the void.

The Chronic Abnormality of Jewish Existence

Labor Zionism was conceptually ill prepared for the persistent abnormality of Jewish existence in Israel. Over the past forty years, Israel has been denied even the prerequisite of normal national existence, that is, recognition by its neighbors. Egypt, the first of its neighbors to offer the possibility of normalization, received the entire Sinai with its oil fields in return – an almost unprecedented concession for the promise of normalization. Egypt's leader, Anwar Sadat, was immediately treated as a pariah among his fellow Arabs, and he eventually paid with his life for the gesture of recognition. His successor has been most cautious in reaching out to Israel.

Nowhere is the surrealistic abnormality of Jewish existence more apparent than at the United Nations, which has passed resolution after resolution condemning Israel, including the infamous resolution equating Zionism with racism – despite the fact that Jews are a multiracial people who permit conversion and who daringly rescued black Ethiopian Jews. Soviet bloc nations and the Arab world have transformed the United Nations into what Senator Daniel Moynihan and Ambassador Jeane Kirkpatrick termed "an international forum for antisemitism." The predominance of the Israel issue in the Security Council and the General Assembly – where no other items (even those threatening world peace) receive half as much attention – underscores the abnormality of contemporary Israeli existence.

Israel is not the only place where Jews retain abnormal status. In the Soviet Union, Jews are persecuted for their religious identity. (In fact, Soviet Jews played a structurally similar role with respect to communists to that assumed by Jews under Christianity – that is, they deny that the messiah has come. By pressing to emigrate, they testify to the fact that Soviet society is not the secular kingdom of God on earth.) Even the Western world has not treated Jews normally. The statement of French prime minister Raymond Barre in the aftermath of the 1980 attack on the rue Copernic synagogue is instructive in this regard. Barre said: "It is unfortunate that the terrorists wanted to kill Jews on their way to synagogue; it is regrettable that innocent Frenchmen were killed instead." Barre contrasted the word "Jew" and the word "Frenchmen" in a country that first granted the Jewish people rights of citizenship in 1789. The word "Jew" was also juxtaposed to the word "innocent," a contrast that was to mark the response of former Austrian chancellor Bruno Kreisky to another attack on a Vienna synagogue only thirteen months later. Kreisky said: "It is the implacable attitude of the Israelis toward the Palestinians that is to blame for these excesses." Kreisky felt that Viennese Jewish worshipers could be held responsible for the behavior of Israelis thousands of miles away in Judea, Samaria, and Gaza. It was psychologically credible for the chancellor to blame the victims' brothers for the attack.

Even American Jewry, whose achievements in a national climate of normalcy have been rightly celebrated,[10] has had uncomfortable moments in the past several years when either domestic or international issues challenged its tranquillity. The oil crisis, American arms sales to Arab countries friendly to the United States but hostile to Israel, the war in Lebanon, the Bitburg controversy, and the Pollard affair were examples of American Jewish discomfort even within an unprecedented context of tolerance and pluralism. Stephen Rosenfeld has written persuasively about antisemitism in American foreign policy; his article, prompted by the 1981 AWACS detection-aircraft sale to Saudi Arabia and the attack on ethnicity in American foreign policy by Charles Mathias, is still relevant today.[11]

Only two segments of the Israeli population were prepared to confront the chronic abnormality of Jewish life: the nationalists and the religious. The former consider antisemitism endemic to gentile society. The latter believe that the religious mission of the Jews as God's people will naturally provoke antisemitism. At Sinai, they teach, *sinah* (hatred) was introduced to the world. Classical political Zionism and its Labor Party descendants, which aimed to transform the Jewish condition in order to end Jewish abnormality, were ill prepared for its failures. The movement could not understand why Israel was not treated as a normal state. Indeed, the hope of normalcy persists even today. Whether taking the form of the Sadat peace initiative or the participation of other Arab countries in negotiations, any movement toward recognition rekindles the dream of normalcy and weakens the power of nationalistic and religious sentiments within Israel. Ironically, a nationalist–religious coalition negotiated the peace treaty with Sadat even though it continued to expect deception.[12] (However, the treaty could be ratified by the Israeli parliament only because Labor Zionists supported it.)[13]

Independence

The Zionist dream of normalization was coupled with a hope for independence. Israel was proclaimed a state at a time when colonial rule was beginning to wane in Asia and Africa. In 1948, Israel was committed to neutrality and self-reliance; it was unwilling to take sides in the major power conflicts dividing East and West and was determined to defend itself in a hostile world. Although Israel's power was limited, a sanguine use of that power was the best guarantee of independence. Within twenty-five years, Israel had achieved regional dominance and survived three wars, fending off attacks in all directions. Yet precisely at the height of power, the Jewish state found itself again dependent on the goodwill of a gentile leader. At a critical moment during the Yom Kippur War, Israel desperately needed an American airlift in order to resupply troops dangerously short of ammunition and basic supplies. For forty-eight hours, the fate of Israel was in the hands of Richard Nixon and his principal advisers – the first secretary of state "of Jewish origin," and a secretary of defense who, although of Jewish ancestry, was a practicing Christian. This shock to Israel's self-esteem cannot be overestimated.[14] Radical dependence was a blow to Israel's ideological expectations and self-confidence. The impact of this dependence has only grown with the years as proud, strong, defiant Israelis have slowly confronted their linkage with the long history of Jewish dependence.

Jews achieved their independence precisely as the world was moving toward interdependence. The key to Israel's survival, its relationship with the United States and the West, lies in the interdependence that marks the geopolitical and defense relationships of the last fifteen years. American friends of Israel sought to recognize this changing reality by pressing for a new understanding of the Israeli-American relationship. In the 1980 presidential campaign, Jewish supporters of all three candidates pressed the nominees to speak of Israel as a strategic asset in the Middle East and the only dependable democratic ally in the region. After some rough starts, including the ill-fated Memorandum of Understanding (M.O.U.) and the ups and downs of Begin's tenure as prime minister, the "strategic alliance" has gained strength and gives concrete expression to the interdependent relationship. A geopolitical and strategic facade for the American-Israeli relationship has supplemented – and perhaps even supplanted – the cultural and moral perspectives that were the basis of previous American commitments. The language of international relations has changed. The perception of Israel as an ally has major political implications and limits the duration and intensity of crises between America and Israel.

The stormy tenure of Begin as prime minister may shed some light on the essential dream of Jewish independence. When the Reagan administration suspended the M.O.U. in response to the extension of Israeli rule to the Golan Heights, Begin responded with a long tirade addressed to then U.S. ambassador Samuel Lewis. Among other things, Begin said that Israel could not be treated as a "banana republic" by the United States, and that the

Jewish people had survived 3,700 years without the M.O.U. and would survive another 3,700 years without it. Throughout the diatribe Begin defiantly, if not arrogantly, reasserted Israeli independence in relationship to Israel's only dependable ally precisely at the moment when he and his supporters were hoping that Israel could be perceived as an interdependent – not dependent – friend of the United States.

Suffice it to say that the dream of independence was dealt a harsh blow by the Yom Kippur War and by the recognition of the complex interdependence of Israel and the United States geopolitically, strategically, economically, and politically. Nevertheless, Israel resents its interdependence and fears dependency on American aid and economic support.

A dialectical politics has developed; Israeli politicians who can resist American pressure or who react defiantly to American statements and policies are rewarded with broad popular support, yet if they are perceived as damaging the relationship substantively, their behavior is regarded with suspicion and testiness. The U.S.-Israel relationship may become strained but not broken. To prove its independence, Israel can never easily acquiesce to an American request.[15]

Vulnerability

Zionism was supposed to end Jewish vulnerability by giving Jews sufficient power to defend themselves. Through the achievement of normal national status, antisemitism was expected to decline. However, for the past four decades Israel has faced implacable Arab adversaries unwilling to recognize its existence. For more than sixty years, ever since the Hebron riots of 1929, Jewish-Arab coexistence in Palestine has been marked by strife and open warfare.[16] Before 1982, after each of the wars Israel emerged stronger than before, more secure and less able to be destroyed. Yet the sense of vulnerability persisted.

The 1981 raid on the nuclear reactor in Baghdad may have illustrated the basic dilemma confronting the Zionist dream of an end to vulnerability; vulnerability may swiftly become the fundamental condition of all nations as irresponsible regimes or terrorist groups gain control of nuclear technology. By bombing the Baghdad reactor, Israel sought to postpone nuclear vulnerability for a decade, by which time possession by nonmajor powers of a nuclear option may well become a worldwide problem requiring an international solution. Yet it is not only nuclear vulnerability and the persistence of Arab antagonism that has dealt the Zionist dream a mortal blow; rather, as events of the War in Lebanon so aptly illustrate, sovereign Jewish existence in Israel has the ability not only to dampen international antisemitism but to arouse it as well. European antisemitism has been gaining wide attention, and although surveys indicate that antisemitism is on the decline in America, Jews are generally convinced that it is increasing.[17]

The politicization of Jewish existence caused by Israel and by economic dislocation can fuel the hatred of Jews. Statements by black power advocates in the late 1960s, the United Nations resolution equating Zionism with racism, and the image of Israel in the media throughout the War in Lebanon and *intifada* have brought an end to the post-Holocaust period when the expression of antisemitism, even if deeply felt, was restrained. In short, Israel has not eliminated Jewish vulnerability; it has altered the context in which vulnerability can be combated.

The Exiles Do Not Feel In Exile

Finally, Zionism envisioned the return of the Jews to the land of Israel and the gradual withering of the diaspora. Since 1948, more than 2 million Jews have moved to Israel. The Jewish population has increased fivefold, from 650,000 in 1948 to 3.5 million today. Nevertheless, the diaspora has not disintegrated. American Jewry has produced a new generation of scholars, teachers, and rabbis to staff its diverse institutions. American Jews are proud and self-affirming; there is little evidence to indicate that the tide of assimilation is insurmountable, that the safety of American Jewry is precarious, or that the attraction of Israel is so great that American Jewry will emigrate en masse.

Conversely, more than 500,000 Israelis (and perhaps as many as 700,000 – that is, nearly 20 percent of the Jewish population of Israel) have left the country, preferring to settle in diaspora communities despite the social stigma of *yeridah* ("descent" from Israel). Zionism underestimated the persistence of the diaspora. Zionism did not account for the fact that Israel stands at the periphery of Western culture and that its sons and daughters who aspire for greater cultural stimulation may be forced to make their way westward – at least for a time, if not permanently. Although central to Jewish culture, Israel remains marginal to world culture.

All immigration movements follow a general push–pull pattern. For large-scale immigration to take place, there must be a push from the native country or a pull to another country that the immigrant finds attractive. In the absence of a push from the West, the pull of Israel attracts the best and the worst of American Jews, that is, those who because of their intense Jewish idealism feel attracted to life in Israel, or those who do not find themselves at home in a pluralistic American milieu. The "pull" of America – its economic, cultural, and intellectual excitement – proves irresistible to many Israelis, at least for considerable time. Furthermore, Israel is also dependent on a strong and vibrant American Jewish community that can argue forcefully and behave politically to enhance American support for Israel. Ideology aside, Israel would be ill served by a withering of the American diaspora even if all American Jews went to Israel.

An Ideological Crisis

Only two segments of Israeli society were prepared for the ideological crisis in the Zionist movement: the nationalists and the religious. The nationalists sensed that antisemitism was less a response to the behavior of the Jew and more a problem endemic to gentile society. They were prepared for an enduring struggle. Their answer to vulnerability was power; their reaction to dependence, defiance. With Menachem Begin as their leader, they were rooted in Jewish tradition and comfortable with its language and symbols at a time when the secular Zionist vocabulary was beginning to lose its power.

For example, the concept of the *land* of Israel has had a long and important place in Jewish tradition. For an exiled people, land was a symbol of past glory and future solace. Religious commandments were dependent on the land; holidays and festivals were observed differently within the land of Israel. By comparison, the concept of the Jewish state and questions of sovereignty, power, and rule have a limited role in Jewish tradition and its emotional matrix. However, throughout the prestate years, Jewish sovereignty and statehood were the goal, the dream of the Jewish population in Palestine. During the first years of the state, *mamlachtiyut* (statism) became an operative political policy pursued relentlessly by Ben-Gurion and the forces he controlled. For the generation coming to maturity after the state was born, a Jewish state was accepted as a normal, natural reality worthy of support, allegiance, and respect, but incapable – except in times of crisis and war – of bestowing a sense of purpose. The land of Israel, on the other hand, echoed the yearnings of centuries and proclaimed a challenge for tomorrow.

Even now, Israel is deeply divided over the question of Zionism's most fundamental value. At stake is whether Zionism is defined as the return of the Jewish people to its land – and hence the land must be retained even if populated by Arabs resistant to Israeli rule – or if Zionism is the reestablishment of a sovereign Jewish state – and hence the state must be preserved by the voluntary sacrifice of land and the deliberate choice not to exercise the historic right of the Jewish people to the land.[18]

The nationalist position has remained relatively consistent over the past three decades. Perhaps the single most dramatic change occurred with the Camp David agreement returning Sinai for the promise of peace with Israel's most powerful neighbor. The religious position has changed more radically, especially after the Yom Kippur War. This shift, coupled with demographic and economic forces, led to the decline of the Labor Party's hold on the Israeli electorate; Maarach finally toppled after twenty-nine years in power.

The religious segment of Israeli society was prepared for the persistent abnormality of Jewish life and for tenacious antisemitism. They could move beyond Labor Zionism as an ideology because religious ideologists never accepted the state as the goal of Zionism. For a very small minority of religious Jews, the Zionist movement is still regarded as a heretical agent of secularization usurping God's prerogative to restore the Jewish people to their homeland. For others, the state is considered a purely secular entity with little transcendent value. No religious significance is attached to it. This position is maintained by Agudat Israel and by Professor Yishayahu Leibowitz, an eccentric but influential Israeli scientist and rabbi who is critical of the religious parties in Israel.[19] It is preferable, the Agudah argues, for Jews to be governed by Jewish rather than gentile rulers. A state controlled by Jews creates some religious difficulties with regard to Jewish law that must be ameliorated, but otherwise the state is of no religious interest.

In addition to the state and the land, a third Zionistic position is reflected in the prayer for the state authorized by the Chief Rabbinate of Israel. The state is referred to as the "dawn of redemption," and this attitude toward Israel is characteristic of many religious Zionists. They differ on the implications of the "dawn" and the meaning of redemption. According to Rav Kook the elder,[20] the state is but a prelude to the building of a sacred Jewish society, the precondition for revolution but not the revolution itself. Rav Kook's vision permitted religious Jews to compromise with secular Zionists by maintaining both the integrity of a religious position and the excitement of an ideological revolution; Kook viewed the state as a necessary but not sufficient precondition for the religious revolution. Kook's concept of Zionism as the dawn of deliverance allowed for the participation of a religious minority within the secular Zionist movement.

Throughout the prestate period and from 1948 to 1973, the religious parties (whether Zionist or avowedly clerical) had limited goals. They sought to maximize the religious observance of the state, to minimize the desecration of traditional religious practices, and to enhance state support for religious institutions (which in turn increased the political patronage the parties could dispense). Religious parties reserved the right to exercise an ideological claim on the greater society but did not pursue their religious agenda with vigor outside the clerical and occasionally the juridical domain. They were in a defensive position, fortifying the status quo against an ascendant secularism. This situation changed in 1973 with the shock of the Yom Kippur War.

Messianic Politics

Yonina Talmon has argued that messianic movements are never the product of catastrophe alone.[21] They are born of an imbalance between expectation and reality, of the disappointments that follow a period of sustained hope. For the Jews, the experience of the past half century has produced quite a buffeting. Jews have endured the epitome of inhumanity as victims of governmental-sponsored and systematically structured mass death in the Holocaust; they have also witnessed the flourishing of hope with the rebirth of the Jewish people in their ancestral land just three years after the destruction. The history of the state was also characterized by cycles of despair and hope – war and armistice, then war and triumph crowned by the return to Jerusalem. The impact of 1967 was startling. The victory created a new reality and a bold, optimistic reaction. The reunification of Jerusalem sparked a reaffirmation of the Jewish past.

For religious Zionists, the 1967 war meant the return of Jewish sovereignty to the ancestral lands, Jewish rule over Jerusalem, and a sense that the state at the dawn of redemption had completed its most significant task. Even the failure of the Arabs to make peace in the aftermath of the war failed to dampen the country's spirit. Therefore, the 1973 Yom Kippur War came as a profound surprise. The war signified a return to vulnerability after a period of invincibility. The realization that Jews were again dependent upon the goodwill of gentile leaders for their very survival provided little comfort. The indecisiveness of the victory that was permitted Israel meant that the country would face harsh choices in an atmosphere of loneliness and isolation that recalled the fate of diaspora Jewish communities. Even the presence of Henry Kissinger seemed to herald the return of the *shtadlan,* the intercessor between Jews and the gentile rulers. Above all, the price that Israel paid for its victory was overwhelming. Some 3,000 Israelis were killed, which in terms of the percentage of the Israeli population would be the equivalent of 225,000 American deaths – and in three short weeks. In the aftermath of the war, a new messianic religious movement gained credibility. Gush Emunim (the bloc of believers) was formed in 1974.

Gush Emunim's attraction for religious Jews, and its power as a Zionist ideology, grew out of a sociological as well as a religious reality. In Israel, there are two parallel – separate but equal – educational systems: a religious educational apparatus and a secular school track. (Ultra-Orthodox Jews maintain yet a third, separate network that is less deferential to the state.) Almost without exception, Orthodox Jews attend religious schools, and they have a separate youth movement that offers many extracurricular activities including field trips and camping. Orthodox Jews may also fulfill their army service in self-contained units designed to allow sufficient time for studying sacred texts. These Orthodox students are taught by a faculty that shares a common orientation, and – as in the Jesuit training of an earlier time – religious school students are in their early twenties before they must encounter secular youngsters with a cognitively dissonant world view.[22] Even neighborhoods have become segregated according to religious practice, so that the atmosphere of the sabbath pervades the street as well as the home and the synagogue.

After the 1973 war, Rabbi Yehuda Amital, the head of Yeshivat Har Etzion (a Talmudic academy set in the Judean desert within the rebuilt Etzion bloc destroyed by the Jordanians in the 1948 war), wrote a penetrating exposition of the new religious Zionist position. Amital's *Hamaalot Memaamakim* (Ascent from the Depths)[23] is a slim, powerful collection of addresses on the meaning of war. Lurking in the background of Amital's thought (and Israeli reality) is the Holocaust, which by its magnitude presents a challenge to even the most devout Jews. How is one to account for such a catastrophe? In a sense, the Holocaust can only be accepted religiously as a prelude to redemption, as the birth pangs of the messiah. Unlike other Orthodox thinkers, such as Rabbi Joseph Soloveitchik[24] who sees Israel as a consoling yet quiet manifestation of divine presence, Amital viewed Israel messianically. His immediate dilemma was to account for the Yom Kippur War.

From the 1967 war, Amital argues, we learned that war can serve a redemptive purpose because – without any desire on Israel's part for the war and following a specific request to King Hussein that Jordan stay out of the war – the Jewish people was restored to the old city of Jerusalem and all its sacred sites. Although the Yom Kippur War at first appears to be an antiredemptive manifestation of history, the opposite may be the case insofar as the Israeli victory was greater than in 1967.

The choice of Yom Kippur as the day to begin the war, Amital reasoned, was an implied attack on Judaism, an assault by Islam against the God of Israel, yet Western nations were the real losers of the war. The false Western god – the idol of technology – was clearly addicted to oil and cheap supplies of energy. Amital argued that Israel's massive victory against powerful armies and overwhelming odds was a great act of divine salvation. The purpose of the war, Amital told his disciples, was to mold the Jewish people into a more solid and spiritually pure unit able to withstand the pressure of the messiah's footsteps. Amital called for the reintensification of efforts, a deepening of commitment equal to the messianic stakes.

Interestingly, Amital was politically astute in his assessment of the West, yet stubborn in his refusal to see the war politically as stemming from concrete grievances and fought for military–diplomatic purposes. Amital returns to the language of presecularized warfare, a language sanctioned by tradition and yet one that classical Zionism sought to overturn. He has further immunized his disciples and their fellow travelers from responding to political pressure, viewing all such compromises as a retreat from a divinely mandated task. Furthermore, Amital was nonapologetic with respect to Israel's position and was unwilling to consider the world in demystified geopolitical terms.

The strength of this ideological perspective should not be overestimated. It is certainly a minority position within the Orthodox community, which itself is in the minority among Israelis. Nevertheless, one dare not overlook its attractiveness or explanatory value. Secular Zionism cannot deal with the continuing enmity of the Arabs toward the Jewish people, with the scope and vehemence of opposition to Israel, and with the persistence of worldwide antisemitism. The goal of an independent state has been reached. Patriotism and statism are not all-encompassing worldviews capable of bestowing a sense of purpose and meaning, especially as the imperfections of an Israeli state are experienced in daily life and exposed by a free press.

Furthermore, Amital's thought intensified – perhaps beyond recognition – values common to the entire society. Secular Zionists also believe that Israel represents the dawn of redemption, and religious Zionists see Israel in messianic terms, yet for both groups the idea is less than dominant and not necessarily understood as the basis for serious politics. Secular Zionism hopes for a revolution within the Jewish people and radical changes in the Jewish situation. Its solution was essentially political. Amital's aspirations were also state-centered, but his means are religious and his solution to the conflict messianic.

Amital's position is even more interesting because he moderated his views considerably after the War in Lebanon. By the time of the 1988 elections, Amital reluctantly led a dovish religious party prepared for political accommodation. Because of the militant patriotism of the *hesder* yeshiva students (those who combined national service with yeshiva study), many of Amital's disciples had volunteered for the elite units of the Israel Defense Forces (IDF), often replacing Labor Zionism's elite, the kibbutzniks. Thus, yeshiva students were on the front line for the war in Lebanon and suffered extremely high casualties. Death became a reality for these students – and their teachers. Amital's response was bold. He subsequently told his students that the Jewish responsibility to the land of Israel must be balanced by commitment to the Torah and people of Israel. If the former is emphasized to the exclusion of the others, then the future of Israel is distorted. While the War in Lebanon may have hardened many positions, it moderated at least one. In response, Amital was ostracized by former political allies.

With the weakening of the secularist-oriented Labor Party and the collapse of the civil religion of Zionism,[25] ultra-Orthodox Jews became increasingly militant and self-confident, demanding greater concessions and support from government, pressing their political and social agenda, and further isolating their homes and children from Israeli society. They have, in part, succeeded with this agenda, but their success has created a backlash. Ultra-Orthodox Jews increasingly live in a social situation that segregates them from other Orthodox Jews and not only from secularists. They, too, have become militant, seeking to preserve the unique character of their life-style, to extend the boundaries of their community, and to insulate themselves from external Israeli society. Recent bus shelter burnings, which provoked an extreme reaction by hostile secularists, who burned a synagogue, may be a prelude of trouble to come.

The revolutionary zeal that characterized Israel's founding generation has been captured by the religious community. The larger society views this development with a combination of admiration and fear. The radical vision has transformed the role of the religious parties, and it has strengthened their demands. Ironically, as a political development, radicalism has weakened the traditional religious parties since Gush followers often prefer more avidly nationalist parties. One result of this shift was the 1984 election of Meir Kahane.

Kahane, an American-born extreme rightist rabbi, was elected to the Knesset after two unsuccessful attempts. Kahane's politics are ultranationalistic. Kahane advocates the gradual expulsion of all Arabs from the land of Israel, first in return for generous compensation and later, if necessary, by force. Kahane unites the religious zeal for a revolutionary change in the behavior and observances of Jews with the nationalists' devout commitment to the land. Yet, unlike the mainstream of both political camps, he offers no allegiance to democracy – at least not a democracy that encompasses Jews and Arabs.

In a sense, Kahane is the ultimate assimilationist. He advocates that Jews treat Arabs the way that Jews were historically treated by Christians and Moslems. Kahane thus tacitly acknowledges Nietzsche's critique of Judaism as the religion of the powerless. Kahane is unable to distinguish between the task of a minority group agitating for rights and recognition by a dominant culture (which will surely tame the more outrageous of the minority's demands) and the responsibility of a majority people, sovereign in their own land. Kahane is fond of saying that only he is willing to follow to the end the logical implications of the nationalist and religious positions.

The divisions we witness in Israel are but a surface manifestation of a deeper struggle over the essential nature of the Zionist revolution in Jewish life. Is the fundamental value of Zionism a return to the *land* of Israel, the flourishing of the *state* of Israel, or the triumph of the *religion* of Israel? Each ideological belief generates its own politics, and every manifestation of Arab zeal and internal strife among Jews fortifies one or another of these positions.

The extremism of Kahane, the lure of messianism, and the militancy of the ultra-Orthodox have reinvigorated mainstream state-oriented Zionist ideologists. Values that were previously regarded as commonplace – such as democracy, pluralism, civility, and tolerance – can no longer be assumed. They must struggle for primacy in the clash of political and civic values.

The accomplishments of secular Zionism are great; they are far more than could have been imagined at the beginning of the century, yet they differ from the original Zionist aspirations. Arab enmity toward Israel and the Kulturkampf among Jews have deepened the divisions, changed the stakes, and transformed the nation. The persistent tensions in the region have fueled the possibility of apocalyptic politics.

13. The Situation of the American Jew

This chapter posits that the events of the 1980s will slowly bring to an end the Israel-centered period for American Jews, leaving in its wake a spiritual and institutional vacuum. Disillusionment may create some distance between the two most significant Jewish communities in the world. Yet, more importantly, vicarious Jewish existence through identification with the State of Israel is not sufficient to nurture another generation of American Jews. Perhaps a more symbiotic relationship will emerge in the future, but in the meantime mutual disappointment may replace inflated expectations.

For the first time since emancipation, the American Jewish diaspora is free to enjoy a public Jewish life and move into the mainstream of American culture without being handicapped by its ethnicity or religious practice. Antisemitism no longer shapes Jewish consciousness or imposes Jewish identity. One can be a Jew in the street – but first one must also rediscover the content of that identity.

After tragedy and triumph, the content of Jewish identity is neither simple nor unidimensional. American Jews have a rich array of possibilities to express their identity rather than one comprehensive worldview that offers community and meaning.

July 14, 1989, was the two hundredth anniversary of the French Revolution. For Jewish history, the French Revolution represents the beginning of a two-century struggle for emancipation – that is, the achievement of equal rights for Jews within the nation state. In France, the battle for emancipation achieved unequal results. Jews became French citizens, yet even a hundred years after the revolution the Dreyfus trial demonstrated that Jews could not receive basic equality under the law.[1] In nineteenth-century Germany, emancipation was regarded as an imposition of the French and hence a source of resentment.

Only in twentieth-century America has emancipation been fully achieved. Unlike any other diaspora Jewish community since the emancipation, American Jews can enjoy a public life without concealing religious identity. For the past two decades, the public life of American Jewry has focused on Israel.

The Six Day War of June 1967 represented a watershed in American Jewish history, inaugurating a twenty-year period in which American Jewish life was Israel-centered. The centrality of Israel reflected itself in the philanthropic life of American Jews. During the Six Day War and the 1973 Yom Kippur War, funds donated to Israel by American Jews increased geometrically, and the threshold of giving established during wartime fervor became the new baseline for community campaigns. Israeli dominance also reflected itself in the institutional life of American Jews. Scores of organizations based their appeal on how much they were doing to sustain the fledgling state. Non-Israel-oriented institutions, such as the American Jewish Committee or B'nai B'rith, took on an ardent pro-Israel agenda. The Reform and Conservative movements started their own Zionist groups, and Jewish camps developed summer programs in Israel. The numbers of pilgrims to Israel increased dramatically, and the heroes of the Jewish people became generals and political leaders (Moshe Dayan, Golda Meir) rather than men and women of intellectual or spiritual achievement. By 1983, the role of Israel had become so dominant that Amos Oz, Israel's most prominent writer, could proclaim to the leaders of the American diaspora gathered at the General Assembly of the Council of Jewish Federations that in the drama of current Jewish history, Israel alone is onstage. "You are the audience,"[2] Oz told American Jews. Few disputed his claim.

This Israel-centered chapter in American Jewish life is drawing to a close. Israel will continue to enjoy strong political support from American Jews, but it will no longer dominate American Jewish consciousness. In part, the reasons are political.[3]

The decade of the 1980s was less heroic for Israel. No raids on Entebbe fired the American Jews' imagination. The Yom Kippur War, in which Israel was attacked on two fronts on the holiest day of the Jewish year, gave way to the 1982 War in Lebanon, a war of aggression and not self-defense. The Jonathan Pollard spy case demonstrated that Israeli intelligence was prepared to exploit, in a sloppy, inept operation, the loyalties that American Jews feel for Israel.[4] The unending struggle of the *intifada,* which pits armed Israeli soldiers against a relatively unarmed civilian population, produced ugly images in the media. Despite Jewish protests of exaggeration and distortion in the news, reports generally reflected the situation on the ground. Furthermore, the generational transition in Israeli leadership from founders to followers, from pioneers to apparatchiks, weakened Israel's mythic hold on American Jewish consciousness.

On the "Who is a Jew?" debate, there was a near break between American Jews and Israel. When the confrontation reached its crescendo, Israel was forced to back down and accept the American diaspora on its own terms. On this issue, the Israeli religious parties sought to delegitimate diaspora Jewry's religious leadership by refusing to recognize the conversions, marriages, or divorces performed by non-Orthodox rabbis, thus challenging the core of Jewish identity in the diaspora. American Jewish leaders refused to allow the Jewish state to demean the integrity of American Jewish identity. As a result, Israel lost influence, and its leadership was demonstrated as inept. This lesson has not been lost on American Jewish leaders.

Israel's overall political situation, which seemingly changes by the hour, has an underlying and rather unpleasant stability. Writing for the *Jerusalem Post,* columnist Allen Shapiro said that "only a confirmed anti-Semite could believe that the people of Israel has the leadership it deserves."[5] Hirsch Goodman, the *Post*'s influential military correspondent, recently wrote: "Israel is at the height of its military power and geopolitical influence precisely as it is at the nadir of its political leadership."[6] American Jewry is not blind to the dearth of Israeli political leadership and the paralysis that has resulted from two successive national unity governments, which were neither national nor unified and could barely govern. Each election, each peace proposal, each change in PLO pronouncements leaves Israel further divided.

A heroic Israel has given way to an impotent political leadership that can neither attract wholehearted American Jewish support nor sustain the mythic weight that a generation of American Jews imposed on Israel when they sought a vicarious basis for their own existence. Israel has lost none of its urgency, none of its necessity as a haven and homeland for the Jewish people, but merely its mythic sufficiency to carry the burden of ultimate meaning for Jewish existence in America, and perhaps in Israel as well.[7]

Yet the reasons for the loss of American Jewry's Israel-centeredness are more than political. Increasingly, it seems that the Holocaust, the undigested trauma of the Jewish people, has left Israel scarred. Despite the prowess of Israel's army, its regional supremacy, its role as an occupying power, and a fifteen-year alliance with the United States, Israel continues to perceive itself as an isolated victim standing alone against overwhelming odds in a hostile world. Even the *intifada,* in which the Palestinians have suffered ten times the casualty rates of the Israelis, has not diminished Israel's sense of itself as a victim of history instead of an actor in it. Over time, this perspective will become ever more dificult for less beleaguered, self-confident, empowered American Jews to share.

The *intifada* has also given rise to the type of extreme or bigoted thinking that had previously been unacceptable among the Israeli populace because of the memory of diaspora victimization. Thoughts are now uttered by recognized political leaders that would have been unimaginable five years ago. Two examples may suffice: A prominent rabbi in Judea publicly asserted that Jewish lives are more valuable than Arab lives and hence that the punishment for taking an Arab life should not be severe. Israel's Ashkenazic chief rabbi later reminded his colleagues that "all men are created in the image of God,"[8] yet no one in the audience who heard the rabbi's original remarks took issue with this violation of Judaism's most basic teaching. Similarly, the IDF chief of staff, Dan Shomron, recently remarked that the *intifada* can be contained only by a political solution or by large-scale deportations.[9] He presumed that because the latter action would be unacceptable (an echo of a not too distant past), the former would be the only possible solution. Shomron may have miscalculated the weight of public opinion.

I am confident that these radical, unacceptable, and, to date, minority opinions in Israel will remain confined to a recalcitrant minority, even if culturally significant and politically influential.

Yet the struggle to combat these views, the very engagement in such radicalism, is spiritually debilitating and alienating for both moderate Israelis and mainstream American Jews.

Structurally, American Jewry is presently less in need of spiritual nurturance from Zion. Day schools, seminaries, graduate programs in Judaica, and communal-service training seminars now provide a cadre of trained professionals for the American Jewish community, people at home as Americans and as Jews. Although Jewish professionals may study for a while in Israel or travel there for conferences and sabbaticals, there is no doubt that their home is in the West. In fact, some of Israel's most successful programs and academic achievements are the product of American-trained scholars who went on aliyah.

The links between Israel and American Jewry are deep and enduring, but American Jews cannot sustain a Jewish life in deferment. Jewish options cannot be restricted to another time or place. Increasingly, American Jews have become assertive and nonapologetic about their choices.

Over the past decade, a new development has taken place in America that may reverse the nature of Jewish communal life since the emancipation. When Napoleon offered equal rights to Jews, his terms were explicit: to the Jews as individuals, everything; to the Jewish community, nothing.[10] That is, Jews could achieve equal rights as citizens of the state, but Jewish communal interests were generally ignored. The poet Judah Leib Gordon articulated the Jewish response to emancipation: "Be a Jew in your home and a man in the street."[11]

For generations, Jewish entry into the larger society required the abandonment of parochial attitudes, practices, appearances, and agendas. One could enter the public domain as a citizen of the state, a professional, an artist, or a scientist, but not as a Jew. If one's Jewishness became publicly apparent, it was usually a handicap. Thus, ever since the emancipation Jews who sought to enter the mainstream of political, intellectual, or cultural life learned to minimize their Jewish identity, conceal it, or deny it altogether. For example, Sigmund Freud feared that psychoanalysis would be stigmatized as a Jewish science and in fact burned his manuscript on Jewish humor. Freud particularly cherished the participation of Carl Jung because of his non-Jewish origins.[12]

Even in America, with its tradition of tolerance and pluralism and the absence of state-sponsored religion, Jewish identity was regarded as disadvantageous. Thus, Walter Lippmann, the distinguished journalist of *The New Republic* and one of America's most influential writers, could comment on every event, but not once did he mention the Holocaust for fear of exposing a parochialism he regarded with shame. Lippmann's behavior was not atypical.[13] In fact, Lippmann blamed the Jews for antisemitism. "The rich and vulgar and pretentious Jews of our big cities are perhaps the greatest misfortune that has ever befallen the Jewish people. They are the real fountain of anti-Semitism."[14] At elite universities such as Harvard or Yale, "joining the club" was a matter of adopting the refinements of the dominant WASP culture and not calling attention to oneself as a Jew.[15]

For the first time, in the past decade American Jews were not reluctant to engage in American public life as Jews. For example, Elie Wiesel and Jacob Neusner have both achieved international prominence as Jews working directly with Jewish material. Contrast Neusner's Jewish identity with that of Harry Austyn Wolfson, the Harvard philosopher who was the most prominent scholar of Judaica in academia for forty years (1920 – 60). Wolfson also wrote anti-Judaic diatribes under a pseudonym for Harvard's Jewish journal. Of his Jewish identity, Wolfson wrote: "Some are born blind, some deaf, some lame, and some are born Jewish."[16]

In political life, an identical process has occurred in which Jewish affiliation and leadership has in no way hampered political ambition. When Stuart Eizenstat was appointed chief of domestic policy for President Jimmy Carter in 1977, he was the highest-ranking practicing American Jew to serve in the White House. A decade later, no one even commented on the religious identity of President Ronald Reagan's chief of staff, Kenneth Duberstein, an ethnic New York Jew.

This new political leadership does not hesitate to affirm their Jewish identity or to advocate Jewish interests. Three examples may suffice. Eizenstat was careful to exclude Iranian Jews from the anti-Iranian presidential orders during the height of the hostage crisis. An observant Jew, Eizenstat was host to the president for Passover seder.

Princeton Lyman is widely credited with initiating the State Department participation in the rescue of Ethiopian Jews. As a midlevel bureaucrat, he did not believe that advancing a partisan cause would hamper his career advancement or that playing it safe would help his career. He skillfully exploited the State Department's memory of inaction to facilitate departmental approval for the rescue. Similarly, Ronald Lauder did not feel inhibited by his religion in dealing with the election of accused Nazi war criminal Kurt Waldheim as president of Austria.

In the past, Jews in political life were cautious about their religious background. If elected, they served from districts with large Jewish populations but were timid about asserting a partisan agenda. In the 1980s Jewish members of the House of Representatives came from Bozorah, Connecticut; Wichita, Kansas; and Dallas, Texas. They represented districts where the Jewish population was less than one-half of 1 percent. Politicians such as Sam Gedjenson of Connecticut (born in a displaced persons camp in Eschwege, West Germany, the child of Holocaust survivors from Lithuania), Ron Wyden of Oregon, and Dan Glickman of Kansas reflect dramatic changes in American Jewry. They have accepted their own Jewishness as a natural part of their identity and wear it as a badge of honor. They take pride in their ethnicity, and their support for Israel is nonapologetic and direct. They respond directly to critics. Barney Frank, another Jewish congressman, from Massachusetts, responded to one of his colleagues who called America a "Christian country" by asking: "If this is a Christian country, what is an overweight Jewish boy from Boston doing up at 5:15 in the morning presiding over the House of Representatives?"

Rudy Boschowitz of Minnesota – a refugee from Hitler's Germany – proudly called himself "the rabbi of the Senate" because of his leadership on Jewish issues. In 1988 Joseph Lieberman from Connecticut was elected to the Senate as an observant Jew, and out of courtesy for his personal religious practice, the Senate Majority Leader has agreed, whenever possible, not to schedule votes on the Jewish sabbath. Frank Lautenberg had served as national chairman of the United Jewish Appeal before running for the Senate from New Jersey in 1982. Howard Metzenbaum was chairman of the Union of American Hebrew Congregations' Social Action Commission before he was elected to the Senate from Ohio.

In the arts and literature, in academia and business, Jews now feel fully at home in America. As Charles Silberman has shown, it may be inappropriate to argue by anecdote, yet the accumulation of anecdotal information can illustrate irrefutable trends. Silberman himself cites an event at Harvard as an example of Jewish acceptance. In 1979 Harvard Hillel moved its quarters. The last day was marked by a procession of the Torahs from the old building to the new. The Dean of Harvard's faculty, Henry Rusovsky (himself a refugee from Nazi Germany) was the featured speaker. He said:

> Today Hillel is moving from the periphery of the campus to its very center. Today let it be said that Harvard welcomed us [in the post-World War II era] with open arms as students and teachers. What is perhaps more remarkable is that we have succeeded in transforming ourselves from a group of individuals into a community; that is really what is being celebrated here today.[17]

The United States Holocaust Memorial Museum is yet another example of American Jewry's movement toward the center of national life. The Museum will be built with private funds donated by the American people, but its creators and builders will primarily be American Jews. The Museum will take what could have been the painful and parochial memories of a bereaved ethnic community and apply them to the most basic of American values. Located adjacent to the National Mall – surrounded by the Smithsonian Institution and the monuments to Lincoln, Jefferson, and Washington – the building and its contents are being designed with the neighbors in mind so that the Holocaust Museum will emerge as an American institution that will speak to the national saga.

Such a mainstream undertaking could not have occurred a generation ago. American Jewry would have been too timid, too ghettoized to share its memories. This Museum could not have been built by survivors alone, but it will not be built without them. Ours is the first generation to stand at a distance from the Holocaust and the last to live in the presence of survivors. The Jewish content of the Holocaust will not be compromised, as some survivors (Elie Wiesel among them) – products of a different generation – feared.

The American Jewish community is a potent political force, able with the help of allies to achieve its political goals: to support candidates helpful to Israel and defeat those who are not; to convince the Congress and successive administrations that aid to Israel is in the vital national interest; and to encourage special efforts on behalf of oppressed Jews in the Soviet Union, Iran, or Ethiopia. This achievement of power is silhouetted against the background of powerlessness and defeat of but one generation ago. American Jews, in the words of Michael Kinsley, live like Episcopalians and vote like Puerto Ricans. They still feel unusual when they are considered part of the "white majority" in the United States.

Israel has contributed much to the renewed pride and self-assertiveness of American Jews. Most Jewish political action – as opposed to political action by Jews – is oriented toward Israel. The American Israel Public Affairs Committee (AIPAC) has come to play an increasingly important role. Its briefings affect Jewish support for political races. Even though AIPAC claims "neither to rate nor endorse candidates," it does publicize voting records with regard to Israel and prioritizes the races each campaign year. It has also spurred the development of pro-Israel Political Action Committees (PACs).

PACs are required by law to operate independently and without coordination, yet the pro-Israel Jewish PACs are part of an informal network whose members often play key roles within other Jewish organizations. Politically inclined Jews gravitate toward AIPAC. Given the centrality of American aid to Israel – which is almost ten times the sum contributed by American Jews – and the lure of mainstream American political figures, AIPAC's success has threatened to overwhelm Jewish defense and philanthropic agencies. Over the past several years, AIPAC has recruited key staff members from other Jewish agencies and has thus taken over their major contacts. American Jewish political operatives have also started to play tough, targeting for defeat elected officials perceived as hostile to Israel.

Increasingly, however, American Jews are less willing to support the politics of annexation and extremism. In 1988 – thirty-six traditional friends of Israel in the United States Senate including such prominent pro-Israel senators as Moynihan (New York), Lautenberg (New Jersey), Boschowitz (Minnesota), Levin (Michigan), and Metzenbaum (Ohio) – wrote an open letter to Prime Minister Yitzhak Shamir advocating that Israel be willing to trade land for peace. Many of the senators were running for reelection. None lost significant Jewish support. In the waning days of the Reagan administration, the American Jewish community did not fight American negotiations with the Palestine Liberation Organization; they were still struggling with the Israeli government on the "Who is a Jew?" issue.

Threats of renewed antisemitic outbreaks have not silenced American Jews. On the contrary, in the aftermath of the Holocaust antisemitism is regarded as the price to be paid for continued Jewish existence; such bigotry is impervious to Jewish behavior – modest or bold, timid or assertive. Thus, Jews feel less inclined to appease antisemites.

The second major influence on Jewish public life has been the civil rights movement, which forced the American people to accept diversity and allow ethnicity an acceptable public identity. Black pride engendered Jewish pride. Black studies on the campus encouraged Jewish studies, and if blacks were breaking the barriers at elite universities, Jewish quotas were soon dropped. If James Baldwin could write of the black experience without being forced into an intellectual ghetto, Elie Wiesel could write of Jewish experience during the Holocaust. The broadening of the American mainstream and the open partnership of blacks, women, and Jews promoted greater freedom for artists to enter the mainstream without denying the particularism of their concerns.

Antisemitism has also decreased for American Jews. It poses few barriers in admission to colleges, graduate and professional schools, or career advancement in industries that had previously been closed to Jews (such as banking or insurance). The creation of meritocracy has facilitated the rise of Jews to prominence in economic and professional life. For example, up until the late 1960s, no Ivy League university had ever had a Jewish president. Since that barrier has been broken, Princeton, Dartmouth, Columbia, and the University of Pennsylvania have all had Jewish presidents. Yale maintained a quota on the admission of Jews until the late 1960s, but less than a decade later the Yale corporation offered its presidency to a Jewish Harvard man. Silberman reports that when Henry Rusovsky turned down the presidency of Yale, his wife asked him if he didn't feel an obligation to accept since he would be Yale's first Jewish president. Rusovsky answered: "I felt we were beyond that. Twenty years earlier that would have been a compelling argument, but not now."[18] Instead, he became the first Jew to turn down the presidency of Yale.

If the rule of emancipation was to "be a Jew in your home and a man in the street," the opposite may be the case for some segments of Jewish life in contemporary America. Many American Jews "are Jews in public"; they serve as presidents of national organizations, head philanthropic campaigns, and chair major Jewish activities, yet they lead private lives fundamentally devoid of Jewish content. It is doubtful that such public roles without inner congruence can sustain another generation. The offspring of such leaders will either develop a personal dimension to their Jewish commitment or more fully assimilate. American Jews will either choose high-intensity Jewish identities or their Jewish identity, devoid of content, will wither away. American Jews today can choose from an unprecedentedly wide array of Jewish options, intellectual, religious, political, and cultural. They can participate in a wide range of Jewish alternatives, or they can opt out of that civilization without penalty. The challenge for contemporary Jews is to find a way to be a Jew in the home that is congruent with one's public position and with the totality of Jewish experience.

Three theorists of modernization may provide insight into the function the inner life must play for American Jews. Benjamin Nelson has argued that modernization is the movement from brotherhood to universal otherhood.[19] Jews, John Cuddihy wrote, have resisted this final stage of modernization and have maintained a remnant of brotherhood.[20] Peter Berger, the distinguished conservative sociologist, has written of the role of mediating institutions – the church, the neighborhood, the family, and the community – in bridging the gap between isolated individuals and overarching, alienating superstructures. Jewishness will find its continued place in the private lives of American Jews in the niche between the atomized individual and the depersonalized larger world. It will endure if it succeeds in becoming a meaningful mediating structure. The breakdown of the family in both its immediate and extended forms has intensified the need for intimate community, and a Jewish structure could also stem the tide of family disintegration by supporting the threatened family unit. Divorce, mobility, patterns of separation (children leaving for college, senior adults moving to the Sun Belt), and prolonged single life mean that the family no longer plays the vital role it once did. The family, as the most basic structure of society, is itself in desperate need of strengthening, and the institutions that bolster the family will have much to offer contemporary Americans. Furthermore, in a world increasingly dominated by *Gesellschaft* (transactional relations) people are in greater need of *Gemeinschaft* (communities based on organic kinship and shared symbols).[21] Experientially rather than ideologically based, a Jewish mediating structure will permit individual growth in a repersonalized environment.

Orthodoxy already provides the single most powerful mediating structure. Because Orthodox Jews must walk to the synagogue, Orthodoxy in America is neighborhood-based. It has become repersonalized with the *shtiebel* (prayer house) replacing the traditional large synagogue, and the parochial school reinforcing the sense of community. *Shtiebels* provide a sense of community, and because they are not professionally led, they allow full participation in the service and in religious life for a well-trained male leadership. However, Orthodoxy continues to deny women a public role in the synagogue, which makes this form of traditional Judaism unattractive or unsatisfying for the majority of American Jews living in a world that has enfranchised women in so many other aspects of public life. In addition, Orthodoxy's certitude of ideological conviction – rare in the contemporary world – comes at an enormous cost: the bifurcation of consciousness and a retreat from the larger world. It is unlikely that more than a small but ardent minority of American Jews will be able to accept the complex network of restrictions and rigidities associated with this way of life.

Within the liberal Jewish community, the Havurah movement has become an accepted appendage of many large synagogues. Like the *shtiebel,* the Havurah provides a strong sense of community and individual participation. Reduced in size, it allows for intimacy and growth. In the words of Martin Buber, the domain of "I–You" is particularly needed in a depersonalized setting where "I–It" relationships are increasingly competitive and fragmented. The Havurah is participatory and generally egalitarian. Even Jewishly undereducated liberal Jews grow in competency as they learn to participate in services. Although some contemporary Jews may be Jewishly illiterate, this generation is the best trained, most highly educated generation of Jews in history and thus uniquely equipped for self-directed study. The deed, the experiential expression of life cycle events or seasonal rhythms – far more than faith or philosophy – becomes the center of Jewish life. For example, the building of a *succah* (a temporary hut for the fall harvest festival) has proliferated in American Jewish life, not because of a return to the law but because it can be built by the family at home with the full participation of each member and can then be used for eating and entertaining guests.

The intellectual life of the American Jews has also enjoyed unprecedented growth. Scholars now teach Judaica on hundreds of campuses. They write quality books of Jewish interest and content each year. An entire literature for learning and self-discovery, for spiritual growth and historical inquiry, has developed in the English language. It is now possible as never before to become a literate Jew without sacrificing one's intellectuality or the quality of learning that one experiences in the professions. Study groups, both formal and informal, have multiplied.

Ironically, the proliferation of Judaic scholars has robbed liberal rabbis of their traditional role. Two generations ago the college-educated English-speaking rabbi was among the best educated of Jews; for immigrant congregants speaking little English, such rabbis also served as representatives to the gentiles. Similarly, a generation ago the non-Orthodox rabbi was the most Jewishly educated of his flock, competent in his field as were the professionals in his congregation in theirs. However, professors of Judaica now often replace rabbis as the repository of Jewish wisdom. Many of today's congregants, products of elite universities with Judaically competent faculty, have studied with the men and women who are writing the books the rabbis are reading. While Christian ministers have been gaining power and political influence, rabbis have been losing power to avowedly secular leaders and to secular learning. Yet the desire for continuing education has only intensified.

Because the average American Jew will spend the first quarter of his or her life in intellectual training (more than 85 percent are college graduates), the process of education is unlikely to end with the choice of career. Especially after the final years of academic investment, when many people begin to experience the limits of where they will grow professionally or find the alienation of the workplace overwhelming, Jewish learning can provide a significant path for spiritual growth.

Education for young philanthropists, for example, begins with an eight to ten-week training session held in the homes of individual members. "Young Leadership" insists on a sustained time commitment in order to become part of the group. Similarly, synagogues have introduced scholar-in-residence study weekends as the highlight of the programmatic year. In Washington, D.C., the Foundation for Jewish Studies has invited distinguished academics to spend semesters in residence giving scores of lectures and classes. To the surprise of many, hundreds of busy professionals included study as part of their weekly calendar of appointments.

A generation ago, American Judaism was characterized by three religious movements: Orthodox, Conservative (including a Reconstructionist branch of the Conservative movement), Reform. Orthodoxy enhanced its position by retreating from the modern world in its pursuit of the past. Conservative Judaism saw itself as normative, as the historical evolution of a tradition that had accommodated to a changing world. Its scholarship probed the historical meaning of a text, its status in a particular time and place. For decades the Conservative Jewish Theological Seminary scrupulously avoided the question of meaning, preferring a value-free "scientific" method of inquiry. Prepared to deal with historical evolution,

Conservative Judaism was ill equipped to grapple with revolution, to deal with a world without precedents, without norms. Responding to the question of historicity, the movement had little to say to the next generation that explored the issue of meaning.

Reform Judaism understood covenantal Judaism as the moral demand for social justice and an ethical world. *Tikkun olam* (mending the world) became its central ideology. Yet, over time, the secular world offered the arena of social action; the civil rights movement, the antiwar movement, the crusades against hunger and poverty, the peace movement, and the human ecology movement became the outlet for such passions. One could fulfill such a covenant without reference to the covenant; one could be a good Reform Jew, according to this approach, without a religious framework.

Reconstructionist Judaism was, to use Charles Liebman's term, "an elite formulation of the civil religion of American Jews."[22] It gave voice to how Jews actually behaved. Its founder, Mordecai Kaplan, explained that American Jews lived in two civilizations: a Jewish civilization with its own language, culture, norms, values, art, music, and literature; and an American civilization. The two could be juxtaposed and reconciled without reference to the transcendent. Kaplan's religious naturalism interpreted everything in this-worldly terms. The task was to demythologize Judaism and make it relevant to the scientific categories and humanistic language of American culture.

For more than a generation, Kaplan's writings of the 1930s and 1940s dictated the course of his movement. Kaplan's views dominated as long as he was alive. In that Kaplan died in 1983 at the age of 102, his work certainly enjoyed a long life span. Within five years of Kaplan's death, the movement shifted ground, naming a neo-Hasidic, liberal, mystically oriented scholar as president of its seminary and thus titular head of the movement. The appointment of Arthur Green (a rabbi ordained by the Conservative movement and the founder of the Havurah movement) represented a turn toward the transcendent. Ironically, Buber may supplant Kaplan as the spiritual godfather of the Reconstructionist movement – and for good reason.

In the post-Holocaust world, the metaphors for speaking about God must be changed. Traditional covenantal language cannot describe the divine–human reality, and metaphors of power and sovereignty have been debased. God as king with Israel as subjects connotes authoritarian rule to people rooted in democratic values, and the agrarian model of God as the shepherd with the Jews as His flock leaves us the sheep who went to the slaughter. Similarly, parent–child images lead to infantilization, and most adults today seek a degree of autonomy and independence rather than the subservience and dependence that characterize traditional liturgy.

A generation ago, Kaplan thought that scientific categories would provide new meaning. He was clearly wrong. His conservative colleagues thought that historical categories would be adequate to sustain tradition, but in revolutionary times history is hardly consoling.

Religious language will be recaptured only by using the interpersonal as a model for the transcendent. The metaphors for speaking of God and tradition will be personal, what Harold Schulweis has described as "predicate theology." Reversing Feuerbach's notion that religion is "the predicate we must make the subject," Schulweis argues that "which is in religion is a subject, we must make the predicate." He continues:

> The aim is not to prove the existence of the subject, but to demonstrate the reality of the predicates. For subject theology, faith is belief in the subject and atheism is denial of its existence. For predicate theology faith is belief in the reality of the predicates and atheism is the denial of its existence. . . . The critical question for predicate theology is not: "Do you believe that God is merciful, caring, peacemaking?" but "Do you believe that doing mercy, caring, making peace are godly?"[23]

A recent article by S. David Sperling provides a second example of relational approaches to the divine. Writing on the oneness of God, Sperling suggested a rereading of the most basic affirmation of Judaism, *shema yisrael adonai elohenu adonai ehad* (Hear, O Israel, the Lord our God, the Lord is One). Sperling suggested that the text be reread, *adonai ehab,* love the Lord.[24] Metaphysical unity is to be replaced by existential embrace. A distinguished Bible scholar, Sperling is certainly not proposing a textual correction of Deuteronomy; he knows how the original source reads. Intuitively, however, Sperling understands the requirements of contemporary religiosity. It is not divine essence but relational quality that is paramount.

In the future, the religious needs of American Jews may not be satisfied by the assurances of Conservative Judaism that history will provide norms and meaning; in the wake of the Holocaust and the difficulties of contemporary Israel, no clear sense of meaning emerges. Nor can the demythologizing of Reconstructionism be persuasive when a desacralized world has proved lethal and vacuous. Remythologizing and a return to the sacred world may be required after everything has been devalued, and remythologizing will begin from the interpersonal and move toward community before it encounters the transcendent.

After tragedy and triumph, the inner life of American Jews cannot but be informed by the momentous events of the recent past. Jews will remain engaged in history, involved with power, and in quest of a spirituality congruent with their complex memories of loss and rebirth. No simple innocence can be feigned.

How do we build on the ashes of Auschwitz? Slowly, tenderly, humanely. With humility, perhaps with hope.

Modern art has developed the collage – fragments pieced together to form a whole whose parts can be in tension, in opposition; the pieces may clash, they may lack coherence, or they may strike a tenuous balance. American Jews are creating just such a collage that will be uniquely their own. It may be too early to understand more than the fragments.

Notes

Preface

1. Michael Berenbaum, *The Vision of the Void: Theological Reflections of the Work of Elie Wiesel* (Middletown, Conn.: Wesleyan University Press, 1979).
2. Milton Himmelfarb, ed., "The Condition of Jewish Belief," *Commentary* 42, no. 2 (August 1966): 71–160.
3. Chaim Potok, "Martin Buber and the Jews," *Commentary* 41, no. 3 (March 1966): 43–49.
4. See Richard L. Rubenstein, "The Meaning of Torah in Contemporary Jewish Theology," in *After Auschwitz: Radical Theology and Contemporary Judaism* (Indianapolis: Bobbs-Merrill, 1966), pp. 113–30.

Chapter 1. The Nativization of the Holocaust

1. See Jacob Neusner, *The Public Side of Learning* (Chico: Scholars Press, 1985), pp. 27–39.
2. Michael Berenbaum, "On the Politics of Public Commemoration of the Holocaust," *Shoah* (Fall/Winter 1981–82): 9, 37. See Chapter 3 of the present volume.
3. President Jimmy Carter's advisers had deep roots in the Jewish community. The Commission was originally suggested in a memo by Mark Siegel, who later left the White House to protest the sale of F-15s to Saudi Arabia. Stuart Eizenstat brought the project to Carter's attention.
4. *Report to the President: President's Commission on the Holocaust* (Washington, D.C.: Government Printing Office, 1979).
5. Charles Liebman and Eliezer Don-Yehiya, *Civil Religion in Israel* (Berkeley: University of California Press, 1983), pp. 151–53.
6. Ibid., pp. 104–7.
7. Gideon Hausner, *Justice in Jerusalem* (New York: Harper & Row, 1966).
8. Henry Kissinger, *White House Years* (Boston: Little, Brown, 1978).
9. Throughout the war Begin kept comparing Beirut and Berlin. Ze'ev Schiff and Ehud Ya'ari report in *Israel's Lebanon War* (New York: Simon & Schuster, 1984) that Begin's basic commitment to the Christian population of Lebanon was a result of his identification with their fate. See also Robert Wistrich, *Hitler's Apocalypse: Jews and the Nazi Legacy* (New York: St. Martin's, 1985), pp. 236–55, entitled "From Berlin to Beirut."

10. Even Kahane's slogans evoke the memory of the Holocaust, and his writings on American Jewry suggest that we are on the brink of another Holocaust.

11. See Charles Liebman and Eliezer Don-Yehiya, *Religion and Politics in Israel* (Bloomington: Indiana University Press, 1984).

12. Sam Bloch, ed., *From Holocaust to Redemption* (New York: American Gathering of Jewish Holocaust Survivors, 1983).

13. See David Wyman, *The Abandonment of the Jews: America and the Holocaust 1941–1945* (New York: Pantheon, 1984).

14. Mary T. Glynn and Geoffrey Bock, with Karen C. Cohn, *American Youth and the Holocaust: A Study of Four Major Curricula* (New York: Zachor, 1982).

15. This definition was expressed in the major address of President Jimmy Carter on the Holocaust and in the decision memo that led to the formation of the United States Holocaust Memorial Council. It is also found in the Executive Order announcing the formation of the Council. (See Chapter 2.)

16. Yehuda Bauer, "Whose Holocaust?," *Midstream* 26, no. 9 (November 1980): 42.

17. *Report to the President*, p. 3.

18. This position is expressed by Eliezer Berkovits in *Faith after the Holocaust* (New York: Ktav Publishing House, 1973).

19. Alvin Rosenfeld, *A Double Dying* (Bloomington: Indiana University Press, 1980), p. 159.

20. Glynn and Bock, *American Youth and the Holocaust*, p. 126.

21. Helen Fein, *Accounting for Genocide* (New York: Free Press, 1979).

22. Terrence Des Pres, *The Survivor: An Anatomy of Life in the Death Camps* (New York: Oxford University Press, 1976), pp. 191–92.

23. Ibid., p. 201.

24. Lawrence Langer, *Versions of Survival: The Holocaust and the Human Spirit* (Albany: State University of New York Press, 1982), p. 79.

Chapter 2. The Uniqueness and Universality of the Holocaust

1. Judah Leib Gordon, "Awake My People!" from *Ha-Karmel* 7, no. 1 (1866).

2. Steven Schwarzschild, "Jewish Values in the Post-Holocaust Future," *Judaism* 16, no. 3 (Summer 1967): 157.

3. Berenbaum, *The Vision of the Void*.

4. Wiesel's experience with the United States Holocaust Memorial Council reinforced his caution. Gypsy representatives first pressed for representation on the Council as one of the Nazis' victims. Once included, the Council member challenged the uniqueness of the Jewish experience, arguing that the Gypsy losses were equivalent to Jewish losses, if not numerically, then proportionally. (In my work as a consultant and later as Project Director of the U.S. Holocaust Memorial Museum, I also encountered a tendency within the professional staff to move from inclusion of non-Jewish victims to a non-differentiation among the victims.)

5. Yehuda Bauer, "Whose Holocaust?", p. 42. Italics added.

6. Walter Laqueur, *The Terrible Secret* (Boston: Little, Brown 1980,), p. 7.

7. Joseph Borkin, *The Crime and Punishment of I.G. Farben* (New York: Free Press, 1978).

8. Richard L. Rubenstein, *The Cunning of History* (New York: Harper & Row, 1975), pp. 1–56.

9. Ismar Schorsch, "The Holocaust and Jewish Survival," *Midstream* 27, no. 1 (January 1981): 38–42.

10. Ibid.

11. Ibid.

12. Eliezer Berkovits, *Faith after the Holocaust*, p. 118.

13. John Cuddihy, "The Holocaust: The Latent Issue in the Uniqueness Debate," a presentation to Zachor: The Holocaust Resource Center's Faculty Seminar, January 1980. The Brown University Judaica series will soon publish a collection of Cuddihy's essays on the Holocaust including this one.

14. Emil Fackenheim, *The Jewish Return into History: Reflections in the Age of Auschwitz and a New Jerusalem* (New York: Schocken Books, 1978), p. 93. Italics added.

15. Robert Alter, "Deformations of the Holocaust," *Commentary* (February 1981). Arnold Jacob Wolf and Michael Berenbaum, "The Centrality of the Holocaust: An Overemphasis?" *The National Jewish Monthly* (October 1980). Jacob Neusner, *Stranger at Home* (Chicago: University of Chicago Press, 1985), *The Death and Birth of Judaism: The Impact of Christianity, Secularism and the Holocaust on Jewish Faith* (New York: Basic Books, 1987), and *The Jewish War Against the Jews: Reflections on Shoah, Golah and Torah* (New York: Ktav Publishing House, 1984); see Chapter 6 of the present volume.

16. Michael Wyschograd, "Faith and the Holocaust," *Judaism* 20, no. 3 (Summer 1971), pp. 293–94.

Chapter 3. Public Commemoration of the Holocaust

1. See *The Gates of Prayer* and *The Gates of Repentance*, edited by Chaim Stern and published by the Union of American Hebrew Congregations (Reform) and *Siddur Sim Shalom* and the *High Holiday Machzor*, Jules Harlow, editor, published by the Rabbinical Assembly and the United Synagogue of America (Conservative). Virtually every Passover *Haggadah* published within the past two decades also contains special readings on the Holocaust as part of the seder.

2. See Irving Greenberg, *The Jewish Holidays* (New York: Summit Books, 1988).

Chapter 4. Two Dialogues

1. The "h" is deliberately lowercase in Weiss's writing.

2. See Irving Rosenbaum, *The Holocaust and Halachah* (New York: Ktav, 1976), p. 9. The Hafetz Hayyim (d. 1933) was one of the greatest spiritual leaders of Eastern European Jewry before the Holocaust.

3. R. J. Zvi Werblowsky, "Faith, Hope and Trust – An Analysis of the Concept of *Bittachon*," *Annual of Jewish Studies* 2 (1964).
4. See Chapter 2.
5. *Babylonian Talmud Yoma*, 69b.
6. Elie Wiesel, "On Jewish Values in the Post-Holocaust Future," *Judaism* (Summer 1967): 285.
7. Irving Greenberg, "Clouds of Fire, Pillars of Smoke: Judaism, Christianity and Modernity After the Holocaust," in Eva Fleischner, ed., *Auschwitz: Beginning of a New Era?* (New York: Ktav; Cathedral of Saint John the Divine; and Anti-Defamation League of B'nai B'rith, 1977), p. 23.
8. Emil Fackenheim, *God's Presence in History* (New York: New York University Press, 1969), p. 84.

Chapter 5. Issues in Teaching the Holocaust

1. Raul Hilberg, *The Destruction of the European Jews: Revised and Definitive Edition* (New York: Holmes and Meier, 1985), p. v.
2. See Michael Berenbaum, "The Inner and Outer World of Hell," *Tikkun* (Fall 1986): 112–15: "When Hannah Arendt wrote the widely publicized *Eichmann in Jerusalem*, Hilberg was lumped together with Arendt and Bruno Bettelheim as one of those who blame the victim for his fate. Hilberg's competence to speak of the Jews was challenged because he does not read the languages of Eastern European Jews. . . . Consequently, his work was dismissed. For more than a decade and a half, he was not invited to speak at Yad Vashem and was at times barred access to its library. . . . A lesser work might have faded into oblivion. . . . A less determined scholar would have turned to another subject. But while good scholarship may be read for a while, great scholarship endures."
3. Kenneth Keniston, *Young Radicals* (New York: Harcourt, Brace & World, 1968), pp. 291–96.
4. Yehuda Bauer, *The Jewish Emergence from Powerlessness* (Toronto: University of Toronto Press, 1979), p. 27.
5. Arthur A. Cohen, *In the Days of Simon Stern* (New York: Random House, 1973), p. 197. Emphasis added.
6. Langer, *Versions of Survival*, p. 79.
7. Yehuda Bauer, *A History of the Holocaust* (New York: Franklin Watts, 1982), and Richard L. Rubenstein and John Roth, *Approaches to Auschwitz: The Holocaust and Its Legacy* (Atlanta: John Knox, 1987).
8. Hannah Arendt, *The Origins of Totalitarianism* (New York: World, 1951), p. viii.

Chapter 7. The Shadows of the Holocaust

1. Rubenstein, *The Cunning of History*, p. 33.
2. Hilberg, *The Destruction of the European Jews*, p. 9.
3. Saul Esh, "The Dignity of the Destroyed," *Judaism* (Winter 1966), reprinted in

Yisrael Gutman and Livia Rothkirchen, eds., *The Catastrophe of European Jewry: Antecedents – History – Reflections* (Jerusalem: Yad Vashem, 1976), pp. 355–56.

4. Hilberg, *The Destruction of the European Jews*, pp. 288–89.

5. As Emil Fackenheim has pointed out in *To Mend the World* (New York: Schocken Books, 1982), the greatest philosopher of the twentieth century, Martin Heidegger, used his stature and prestige of office to eliminate Jews from German universities.

6. Borkin, *The Crime and Punishment of I.G. Farben*.

7. See William Styron's introduction to the 1978 edition of Richard L. Rubenstein's *The Cunning of History*, and Rubenstein and Roth's *Approaches to Auschwitz*.

8. Rubenstein, *The Cunning of History*.

9. In a society without rapid progress, a person may face the same problems that confronted his grandparents; not so in a society where the pace of change is rapid. Each generation confronts unprecedented problems, and each must search afresh for wisdom.

10. Hilberg, *The Destruction of the European Jews*, chap. 10.

11. Victor Frankl, *Man's Search for Meaning* (Boston: Beacon Press, 1963).

12. Emil Fackenheim, *To Mend the World*.

13. Rubenstein, *The Cunning of History*, p. 25.

14. See Greenberg, "Clouds of Smoke, Pillars of Fire."

15. David Biale, *Power and Powerlessness in Jewish History* (New York: Schocken Books, 1986), p. 210.

16. During a trip to Israel in the middle of *intifada*, I was struck that many Israelis felt themselves to be victims of the *intifada* despite a casualty ratio of ten Palestinians to every Israeli killed or injured.

17. This letter was addressed to A. Leon Kubowitzki of the World Jewish Congress. For a complete text, see David S. Wyman, *The Abandonment of the Jews*, p. 296.

18. Address to the United Jewish Appeal Young Leadership Conference on March 14, 1988. Netanyahu, an expert on terrorism, is Israel's Deputy Foreign Minister.

19. See Chapter 12.

Chapter 8. Franz Rosenzweig and Martin Buber Reconsidered

1. Chaim Potok, "Martin Buber and the Jews," pp. 43–49.

2. Ibid., p. 49.

3. Ibid.

4. Milton Himmelfarb, ed., "The Condition of Jewish Belief," pp. 71–160.

5. Ibid., p. 72.

6. Nahum Glatzer, *Franz Rosenzweig: His Life and Thought* (New York: Schocken Books, 1953).

7. Eugen Rosenstock-Huessy, ed., *Judaism Despite Christianity* (University: University of Alabama Press, 1969).

8. Franz Rosenzweig, *The Star of Redemption* (New York: Holt, Rinehart & Winston, 1971), translated from the second edition of 1930 by William W. Hallo.

9. For an assessmant of the dialogue, see the introductory essays in *Judaism Despite Christianity* by Harold Stahmer, Alexander Altmann, and Dorothy Emmet, pp. 1–71.

10. Both Arthur A. Cohen and Richard Rubenstein have written psychoanalytically oriented essays that probe the conflicting influences at war in Rosenzweig. While Cohen emphasizes the impact of Franz Rosenzweig's father, Rubenstein analyzes the mother's role. Both essays are instructive, revealing alternate dimensions of Rosenzweig's experience. See Arthur A. Cohen, "Franz Rosenzweig's *The Star of Redemption:* An Inquiry into Its Psychological Origins," *Midstream* 18, no. 2 (February 1972); and Richard L. Rubenstein, "On Death in Life: Reflections on Franz Rosenzweig," *Soundings* 55, no. 2 (Summer 1972).

11. *Judaism Despite Christianity,* p. 113.

12. Glatzer, *Franz Rosenzweig,* p. 342. (Excerpts from a letter written to Rudolph Ehrenberg.)

13. Ibid., pp. 342–43.

14. *Judaism Despite Christianity,* p. 136.

15. For example, see Buber's essay "Two Foci of the Jewish Soul," reprinted in Martin Buber, *Israel and the World* (New York: Schocken Books, 1948), pp. 28–41, especially pp. 28–29.

16. Exodus 19:20.

17. For a survey of the legendary material, see Louis Ginzberg, *Legends of the Jews,* vol. 3 (Philadelphia: The Jewish Publication Society of America, 1911), pp. 77–144. For a contemporary Orthodox position, see J. B. Soloveitchik, "The Lonely Man of Faith," *Tradition* 7, no. 2 (Summer 1965).

18. Martin Buber, *On the Bible* (New York: Schocken Books, 1967), pp. 77–78. Also see Benny Kraut, "The Approach to Jewish Law of Martin Buber and Franz Rosenzweig," *Tradition* (Summer, 1972).

19. Martin Buber, *I and Thou,* translated by Walter Kaufmann (New York: Scribner, 1970), p. 147. Translation copyright © 1970 Charles Scribner's Sons. Reprinted with permission of Charles Scribner's Sons, an imprint of Macmillan Publishing Company.

20. Martin Buber, *On Judaism* (New York: Schocken Books, 1967), p. 150.

21. Buber, *I and Thou,* p. 167.

22. Franz Rosenzweig, *On Jewish Learning* (New York: Schocken Books, 1955), p. 85.

23. Gershom Scholem, "Religious Authority and Mysticism," *Commentary* 38, no. 5 (November 1964): 31–40, reprinted in Scholem, *On the Kabbalah and Its Symbolism* (New York: Schocken Books, 1969), pp. 5–32.

24. Marshall Sklare, "The Greening of Judaism," *Commentary* (December 1974): 54. Italics added.

25. Arthur Waskow, "Sex, Marriage, the Havurot, and Halachah," *Kesher* (June 1975).

Chapter 9. The Problem of Pluralism in Contemporary Orthodoxy

1. See Janet Aviad, *Return to Judaism: Religious Renewal in Israel* (Chicago: University of Chicago Press, 1983), and Adin Steinsaltz, *Teshuvah: A Guide for the Newly Observant Jew* (New York: Free Press, 1987), Hebrew edition first published in Israel in 1982.
2. Reuven P. Bulka, ed., *Dimensions of Orthodox Judaism* (New York: Ktav, 1983), pp. 5–33.
3. See Charles Silberman, *A Certain People: American Jews and Their Lives Today* (New York: Summit Books, 1986); Leonard Fein, *Where We Are: The Inner Life of America's Jews* (New York: Harper & Row, 1988); Calvin Goldscheider and Alan Zuckerman, *The Transformation of the Jews* (Chicago: University of Chicago Press, 1984), pp. 172–88.
4. Joseph Soloveitchik, "Kol Dode Dofek," in *In Aloneness, In Togetherness* (in Hebrew), edited and with an introduction by Pinchas A. Pelí (Jerusalem: Orot, 1976). Irving Greenberg translates *brit yeud* as "the covenant of destiny." I prefer David Hartman's translation but will use the two interchangeably, especially when referring to Greenberg's writing.
5. Jean-Paul Sartre, *Anti-Semite and Jew* (New York: Schocken Books, 1965), translated by George J. Becker.
6. See S. Z. Abramov, *Perpetual Dilemma: Jewish Religion in the Jewish State* (Teaneck, N.J.: Fairleigh Dickinson University Press, 1976).
7. *Ha'aretz,* January 17, 1985. The injunction against selling land in Israel to non-Jews was based on Deuteronomy 7:2 as explained by Maimonides in *Hilchot Avodah Zarah VeHukot Hagoyim* (chap. 10:4), cited by Yehoshafat Harkabi, "Judaism: A Call for a Change" (an unpublished manuscript that is a revised and enlarged version of Harkabi's presentation to the Council of Reform and Liberal Rabbis at the Liberal Jewish Synagogue in London, May 26, 1987).
8. *Ha'aretz,* October 23, 1979, cited by Harkabi.
9. See Maimonides, *Hilchot Avodah Zarah VeHukot Hagoyim* (chap. 7:1), cited by Harkabi.
10. "Atlanta Brave: Trying Times for Israel's Arab Counsel," by Lisa Hostein in *Washington Jewish Week* 24, no. 5 (February 4, 1988).
11. See Harkabi, "Judaism."
12. John Cuddihy, *No Offense: Civil Religion and Protestant Taste* (New York: Seabury Press, 1978).
13. Silberman, *A Certain People,* and Fein, *Where We Are.*
14. See Zvi Yaron, *The Teachings of Rav Kook* (in Hebrew) (Jerusalem: World Zionist Organization, 1974), and Michael Berenbaum in Richard Rubenstein, ed., *Spirit Matters* (New York: Paragon Press, 1987), pp. 187–208.

15. See Larry Yudelson, "Orthodox Rabbis Fume: What Ties with Other Jews?" in *Washington Jewish Week,* May 28, 1987.

16. Address to Center for Leadership and Learning conference on Jewish Unity in Princeton, New Jersey. See a report of the conference and the text of Norman Lamm's address "Unity and Integrity," *Washington Jewish Week,* March 27, 1986, and Michael Berenbaum, "Will There Be One Jewish People in the year 2000?: Leaders Put Forth Bold Programs," ibid.

17. Several of Soloveitchik's works have appeared in English, including: *Halakhic Man* (Philadelphia: The Jewish Publication Society, 1983); *The Halakhic Mind: An Essay on Jewish Tradition and Modern Thought* (New York: Free Press, 1986); Pinchas Peli Hacohen, *Soloveitchik On Repentance* (New York: Paulist Press, 1984); Soloveitchik, *In Aloneness and In Togetherness; Five Addresses,* translated by S. M. Lerhman and A. H. Rabinowitz, edited by Zvi Faier (Jerusalem: Tal Orot Institute, 1983); *Reflections of the Rav: Lessons in Jewish Thought* (adapted from lectures by Rabbi Joseph Soloveitchik) by Abraham R. Besdin (Jerusalem: The World Zionist Organization, 1979). Soloveitchik's major articles include: "The Lonely Man of Faith," in *Tradition,* "Confrontations," "The Community," "Majesty and Humility," "Catharsis," "Redemption, Prayer, Talmud Torah," and "A Tribute to the Rebbitzen of Talne."

18. Soloveitchik, *Halakhic Man,* p. 19.

19. Ibid.

20. See Irving Greenberg, "Will There Be One Jewish People by the Year 2000?" in *Perspectives* (CLAL pamphlet), p. 3.

21. Lamm, "Unity and Integrity."

22. Irving Greenberg, "Toward a Principled Pluralism," in *Perspectives* (CLAL pamphlet), p. 28.

23. Irving Greenberg, "Voluntary Covenant" (a pamphlet of The National Jewish Resource Center, 1982), p. 4.

24. Ibid., p. 7.

25. Ibid.

26. Irving Greenberg, "Cloud of Smoke, Pillar of Fire," in Fleischner, ed., *Auschwitz: Beginning of a New Era?,* p. 23.

27. David Hartman, *The Living Covenant: The Innovative Spirit in Traditional Judaism* (New York: Free Press, 1985), p. 12.

28. Ibid., pp. 232–33.

29. Ibid.

Chapter 10. The Journey of Elie Wiesel

1. Robert MacAfee Brown, *Elie Wiesel: Messenger for All Humanity* (Notre Dame, Ind.: University of Notre Dame Press, 1984), John Roth, *A Consuming Fire* (Atlanta: John Knox, 1980), and Berenbaum, *The Vision of the Void.*

2. Elie Wiesel, *The Town Beyond the Wall* (New York: Holt, Rinehart & Winston, 1964), p. 118.

3. Irving Abrahamson, *Against Silence: The Voice and Vision of Elie Wiesel* (New York: Holocaust Library, 1985).
4. *Report to the President: The President's Commission on the Holocaust*, p. iv.
5. Wiesel's response to the Palestinian uprisings of 1987–89 has been to reaffirm his love for Israel and to ask – ever so gently – if Israel did not make some mistakes in its handling of the Arab problem.
6. Buber, *I and Thou*, pp. 89–90. Emphasis added.

Chapter 11. Jacob Neusner and the Renewal of an Ever-dying People

1. Jacob Neusner, *Death and Birth of Judaism*, p. 72.
2. Ibid., p. 335.
3. Ibid., p. 340.
4. Ibid., p. 342.
5. Ibid., pp. 348–49.

Chapter 12. Political Zionism and Its Would-Be Successors

1. S. Z. Abramov's *Perpetual Dilemma* is the best treatment of religion in Israel. Unfortunately, Abramov (the former deputy speaker of Israel's parliament) completed his work before the declericalization of the religious parties and their consequent impact on mainstream politics.
2. A recent work by Ian Lustick, *For The Land and the Lord* (New York: Council on Foreign Relations, 1988), is a significant exception to this rule in that it explores the ideological role of religious extremism in mainstream Israeli politics.
3. See Howard R. Penniman, ed., *Israel at the Polls: The Knesset Elections of 1977* (Washington, D.C.: American Enterprise Institute, 1979), for an excellent discussion of the changes in the Israeli electorate.
4. See Amos Elon, *Herzl* (New York: Holt, Rinehart & Winston, 1975), and Alex Bein, *Theodore Herzl* (New York: Athenaeum, 1970), as well as Arthur Hertzberg, *The Zionist Idea* (New York: Athenaeum, 1969).
5. Mordecai Kaplan, *Judaism as a Civilization* (New York: Macmillan, 1935), reissued by the Jewish Publication Society in 1982 in honor of Professor Kaplan's hundredth birthday.
6. Jacob Neusner, *From Politics to Piety* (Englewood Cliffs, N.J.: Prentice-Hall, 1973).
7. See my discussion of Rosenzweig in Chapter 7 of this volume.
8. Even the early Israeli treatments of the Holocaust were designed to recover the heroic posture of the ghetto fighters and resistance warriors. Israelis were uncomfortable with the history of Jew as victim. See Yehuda Bauer, *The Jewish Emergence from Powerlessness* and *The Holocaust in Historical Perspective* (Seattle: University of Washington Press, 1978), pp. 30–50.
9. Earl Raab, "Anti-Semitism, a Fact and a Commodity – 1982," unpublished manuscript.

10. Silberman, *A Certain People: American Jews and Their Lives Today*, and Fein, *Where We Are*.

11. Stephen Rosenfeld, "Dateline Washington: Anti-Semitism in U.S. Foreign Policy," *Foreign Affairs* (Summer 1982).

12. Paul Eidelberg, *Sadat's Strategy* (Dollard Des Ormeaus, Quebec: Dawn, 1979).

13. Israeli leaders, such as Prime Minister Yitzhak Shamir and Defense Minister Moshe Arens who in 1989 asserted that the Camp David agreement is the basis for Arab-Israeli negotiations, voted against the accords in 1979.

14. Amia Lieblich, *Tin Soldiers on a Jerusalem Beach* (New York: Pantheon, 1978).

15. The first meeting between an Israeli leader and the American president is always tension-filled. In the midst of the *intifada*, Prime Minister Shamir invited world Jewish leaders to Israel for a demonstration of solidarity before he went to Washington to meet with President George Bush.

16. Netanel Lorch, *One Long War: Arab Versus Jew since 1920* (New York: Herzl Press, 1976).

17. See Raab, "Anti-Semitism."

18. Uriel Tal, "The Land and the State of Israel in Israeli Religious Life," in *The Rabbinical Assembly Proceedings 1976* (New York: The Rabbinical Assembly, 1977).

19. Yishayahu Leibowitz, *Judaism, the Jewish People and the State of Israel* (In Hebrew) (Tel Aviv: Schocken Books, 1975).

20. Even Rav Kook's famous analogy equating the building of Israel by the pioneering generation with the construction of the Holy of Holies in the ancient Temple considers Zionism as a prelude to the religious revolution and merely defers the Kulturkampf until all immediate tasks have been completed. His son and disciple understood the contradictions in his father's thought and refused to defer the crisis much longer. See Zvi Yaron, *The Teachings of Rav Kook*.

21. Yonina Talmon, "The Pursuit of the Millennium: The Relations between Religion and Social Change," in Norman Birnbaum and Gertrud Lenzer, eds., *Sociology and Religion* (Englewood Cliffs, N.J.: Prentice-Hall, 1969), pp. 238–54.

22. Abramov, *Perpetual Dilemma*, pp. 224–64.

23. Yehuda Amital, *Ascent from the Depths* (in Hebrew) (Jerusalem: Alon Shevut, 1974).

24. Soloveitchik, *In Aloneness, In Togetherness*, pp. 331–400.

25. Charles Liebman and Eliezer Don-Yehiya, *Civil Religion in Israel*.

Chapter 13. The Situation of the American Jew

1. Arendt, *Origins of Totalitarianism*, pp. 89–123; Rubenstein and Roth, *Approaches to Auschwitz*, pp. 66–88; and Arthur Hertzberg, *The French Enlightenment and the Jews: The Origins of Modern Anti-Semitism* (New York: Columbia University Press, 1968).

2. Amos Oz, an address to the General Assembly of the Council of Jewish Federations' meeting in Atlanta. Despite Oz's strong dissent from the War in Lebanon and his criticism of the contemporary Israeli policy, he reiterated his Zionist critique of American Jewry in speeches throughout the United States.

3. By margins of more than two to one, American Jews endorse a generally "dovish" position on Israel, yet this does not directly affect their basic support for Israel. See Fein's *Where We Are*, chap. 6.

4. See Wolf Blitzer, *Territory of Lies* (New York: Harper & Row, 1989).

5. *Jerusalem Post*, November 6, 1986.

6. *New York Times*, July 11, 1989.

7. In a review of Thomas L. Friedman's *From Beirut to Jerusalem*, Martin Peretz wrote: "As a boy Israel made him [Friedman] proud, stiffened his spine, filled him with a tribal feeling. Like most tribalists, he thought his tribe was perfect. It wasn't until he went to Israel in the 1980s, he says in a startling confession of naivete and ignorance that he 'discovers that it isn't the Jewish summer camp of his youth.' This discovery simply busted his Zionist heart. . . . "I was myself a passionate child Zionist too," Peretz wrote, "but I knew very few others whose Israel was so unrealistic, so unnerving, so unflawed as Friedman's. Those I knew grew up." *The New Republic* (September 4, 1989): 37.

   Yet as they grew up, they became less passionate about Israel, which meant something else to them, something less to them, than it did in their youth.

8. See "Chief Rabbi Speaks Out," *Jerusalem Post* (International Edition), June 6 1989.

9. "Force Can't End the Uprising," ibid. (International Edition), June 24, 1989.

10. See Arendt, *Origins of Totalitarianism*, p. 29.

11. Judah Leib Gordon, "Awake My People."

12. David Bakan, *Sigmund Freud and the Jewish Mystical Tradition* (New York: Schocken Books, 1965); Paul Roazen, *Freud and His Followers* (New York: New American Library, 1971); John Murray Cuddihy, *The Ordeal of Civility: Freud, Marx, Levi-Strauss and the Jewish Struggle with Modernity* (New York: Basic Books, 1974), p. 77.

13. See Stephen J. Whitfield, "From Publick Occurrences to Pseudo-Events: Journalists and Their Critics," *American Jewish History*, 72, no. 1 (September 1982), and Ronald Steel, *Walter Lippmann and the American Century* (New York: Vintage Books, 1981).

14. "Public Opinion and the American Jew," *American Hebrew* (Spring 1922).

15. See Dan A. Oren, *Joining the Club: A History of Jews and Yale* (New Haven, Conn.: Yale University Press, 1985); and Marcia Graham Synnott, *The Half Opened Door: Discrimination in Admissions at Harvard, Yale, and Princeton, 1900–1970* (Westport, Conn.: Greenwood Press, 1979).

16. H. A. Wolfson, "Escaping Judaism," *Menorah Journal* 7, no. 3 (August 1921). See Hillel Goldberg, *Between Berlin and Slobodka: Jewish Transition Figures From Eastern Europe* (Hoboken, N.J.: Ktav Publishing House, 1989), pp. 37–62.

17. Silberman, *A Certain People,* p. 101.
18. Ibid.
19. Benjamin Nelson, *The Idea of Usury: From Tribal Brotherhood to Universal Otherhood* (Chicago: University of Chicago Press, 1949).
20. Cuddihy, *The Ordeal of Civility,* pp. 3–14.
21. Ferdinand Tonnies, *Community and Society* (New York: Harper Torchbooks, 1965).
22. Charles Liebman, *The Ambivalent American Jew* (Philadelphia: The Jewish Publication Society, 1973), pp. 43–87.
23. Harold M. Schulweis, *Evil and the Morality of God* (Cincinnati: Hebrew Union College Press, 1984), p. 122.
24. S. David Sperling, "The One We Ought to Love," in Eugene Borowitz, ed., *Ehad: The Many Meanings of God is One* (Port Jefferson, N.Y.: Sh'ma, 1989), p. 85.

Index

academia (U.S.): Jews in, 4, 163
Accounting for Genocide (Fein), 25
actuality, 96, 100
Against Silence (Wiesel), 120
Agnon, S. Y., 47, 50–1
Agudat Israel, 149
Akiva, Rabbi, 44
Algeria, 45
Alter, Robert, 27, 175
American Academy of Religion, xx
American culture, 4, 9, 170; Holocaust in, 5–6, 13, 17; Jews in, 156
American dream, 9
American Gathering of Jewish Holocaust Survivors, 8–9
American Israel Public Affairs Committee (AIPAC), 164
American Jewish Committee, 157
American Jewish community, 90–1; Israeli dependence on, 147
American Jewish life: Holocaust in, 43–60, 126
American Jewry (Jews), xvii–xix, 4, 76, 86, 129, 146; abnormality in existence of, 142–3, 148; activist, 83; Buber and Rosenzweig and, 90–1; children of, 68, 102; connection with fellow Jews, 83; effect of Holocaust on, 3, 4, 16 82; inner life of, 166–8; institutional life of, 157, 167; intellectual life of, 168–9; Orthodoy in, 101–3, 104, 105; philanthropy, 157, 169; political support for Israel, 157, 164–5; professionals in, 160; and public commemoration of Holocaust, 33; relation with Israel, 70, 91, 160; situation of, 105, 132, 156–72; E. Wiesel and, 118
American Judaism of Holocaust and redemption, 117, 130, 132–3
American Youth and the Holocaust (Glynn and Bock), 11
Americanization of Holocaust, 8–13, 20–2, 25, 41
Amital, Yehuda, 153; *Hamaalot Memaamakim*, 151–2

Anielewicz, Mordecai, 9
anomie, 89; in Buber, 90, 98
Anti-Defamation League, 45
anti-God, 119, 121
antisemitism, 7, 19, 21, 71, 80, 82, 95, 152, 156; and American Jews, 165, 166; Christian, 94; decline of, xvii, 140, 145; endemic in gentile society, 147; European, 136, 146; Holocaust different from previous manifestations of, 29, 48–9, 67, 72–3; international, 22; in Jewish consciousness, 27; and Jewish identity, 102–3; Jews blamed for, 161; normalization in ending, 139; Israeli state and, 140, 143, 146, 148; in United Nations, 141
apocalypse, 86
apocalyptic messianism, 8
apocalyptic politics, 134
Arab-Jewish wars, 134
Arabs, xix, 8, 148, 150, 152, 155; expulsion of (proposed), 154; and Jewish vulnerability, 145–6
Arafat, Yasir, 45, 49n, 84
Arendt, Hannah, 23, 30, 63, 137; *Origins of Totalitarianism, The*, 67
Argentinean Jewry, 85
Armenian genocide, 10, 25, 32, 37, 38
army (Israel), 42, 131, 137, 159
arts (U.S.) : Jews in, 163
assimilation, 92, 115, 146, 154
Auschwitz, 12, 16, 27, 46, 66, 75, 121, 172; covenant after, 58; God and, 67, 113; optimism and reality of, 13–16; as perverse perfection of slavery, 24; U.S. failure to bomb, 9, 82
authority, 70
Auto-Emancipation (Pinsker), 135–6

baal teshuvah movement, 102
Babi Yar (memorial), 21
Babylonia, 80
Baghdad reactor bombing, 145–6
Bahais (Iranian), 125
Baldwin, James, 165